SMALL SCALE IRRIGATION
A Manual of Low-cost Water Technology

Peter H. Stern

Intermediate Technology Publications Ltd/
International Irrigation Information Center

Acknowledgements

We are indebted to the joint working party of the Inter-mediate Technology Development Group's Water and Agriculture Panels for help in deciding on the subject matter of this book and for comments on the text. We thank Mr J.R.E. Hindson for the information about contour seepage furrows in Chapter 4, Mr R.A. Collett for the technical content of Appendices B, C and D, and Mr G.P.C. Henry for the edited case study in Appendix E-1. We are grateful to Mr Paul Harrison for permission to reproduce the article in Appendix E-II. We are also grateful for having been able to draw on information from the FAO Irrigation and Drainage Paper 24, 'Crop Water Requirements', and on the FAO Development Papers 88 'Sprinkler Irrigation' and 95 'Surface Irrigation'. Where illustrations and drawings have been supplied from other sources, credits are acknowledged beside each item. Our cover picture is from a photograph by Douglas Dickins.

Grateful thanks are conveyed to Professor H. Shalhevet and to other referees who scrutinised the text and made many useful and helpful suggestions.

Published jointly by Intermediate Technology Publications Ltd, 9 King Street, London WC2 8HN, U.K. and the International Irrigation Information Center, Volcani Center, P.O.B. 49, Bet Dagan, Israel; P.O.B. 8500, Ottawa, K1G 3H9.

Published 1979
Reprinted 1980
Reprinted 1982
Reprinted 1984

ISBN 0 903031 64 7

Printed by the Russell Press Ltd, Gamble Street, Nottingham NG7 4ET. Telephone: (0602) 74505.

Contents

Tables

Figures

Preface

This handbook has been written for all who are concerned with the development of irrigated cultivation on a small scale and with limited technical and financial resources. Some of the readers, I hope, will be the farmers themselves, but because the book is in English, it is primarily intended for district officers, extension and community development agents, volunteers and other operators, trained in English to Diploma level or the equivalent, working in rural areas and usually out of reach of much of the technical paraphernalia and know-how readily available to professionally trained people.

Often, in my experience, small rural communities think about irrigation and sometimes embark on irrigation projects without fully appreciating the problems involved, or the extra demands which a change-over from rain-fed to irrigated cultivation will make on their time, labour and resources. The first part of this book is an attempt to look at some of these problems.

"What is 'small-scale' and how low is 'low cost'?", it may justifiably be asked. In one country I visited recently the government described small irrigation projects as those between 100 and 1,000 hectares. In this book, 100 hectares has been taken as the extreme upper limit, 2 to 20 hectares as the range of sizes for most small farm units in the developing world, and even a one-tenth hectare vegetable plot is a viable irrigation unit for a family under certain conditions.

On the question of cost, 'low cost' is a very relative term, depending on local economic circumstances, and no attempt is made to define it. When a large project is so costly that no major international funding agency will finance it, the conclusion that nothing can be done seems negative and inadequate if, by introducing more appropriate technology which makes better use of local resources, the project can be made feasible. A scale of expenditure which may be well within the means of a rural community in one country will be too costly in another. Sprinkler irrigation is too expensive for small-scale farming in most developing countries, but may be feasible in some, and therefore it has been included.

The second and third parts of the book are devoted to the technical aspects of irrigation. In the knowledge that many readers will not have had a scientific education, technical matter has been treated as simply as possible. Inevitably some sections, and especially those dealing with the theories of crops, soil and water, and the design of channels and pipe lines, will be meaningful only to readers who have some mathematical and scientific background, and those sections will confound others. At the same time professional readers may be disturbed at some of the over-simplications. These are risks which have to be taken in this attempt to fill a gap in the communication of knowledge. For those who want further reading on some of the subjects, suggested books are listed at the end of the more technical chapters.

Peter H. Stern

PART I
THE IRRIGATION SCENE

Chapter 1
Introduction

What is Irrigation?

It may at first sight appear to be unnecessary to define an activity which is well-known in a great many countries. But in this book we shall be talking about irrigation in its widest sense, and because this takes us beyond the limits of what is commonly understood to be irrigation, we shall begin with a definition. *Irrigation* is any process, other than natural precipitation, which supplies water to crops, orchards, grass or any other cultivated plants. Thus we shall include run-off farming, humid culture, and micro and manual irrigation, because these are important and significant features of small scale development. We shall not include fish farming, which though a valuable use for land and water, is outside the scope of this book.

Water and Agriculture

Every farmer knows that cultivation requires air, soil, water and sunshine, or to put it more scientifically, the essential inputs to the growth of vegetation are plant nutrients, water and energy. In the wetter parts of the world, where rain-fed cultivation is practised, the farmer's activities consist of selecting suitable (that is fertile) land, preparing the soil for cultivation, and sowing, tending and harvesting his crops. Natural rainfall provides the water needed. But in many other places otherwise favourable for cultivation, natural rainfall does not provide all the water needed, and irrigation can make up this deficiency.

In arid and semi-arid regions, there is usually little doubt about the need for irrigation. Most of the world's great irrigation developments are to be found in these regions. Large engineering works on major rivers such as the Nile at Aswan, Egypt (Figure 1), provide water to distribution systems serving thousands of people and tens of thousands of hectares (Fig. 2). Also in these regions there is a very large number of small irrigation schemes, farmed and operated by traditional methods which have been passed down from antiquity.

Fig.1 The Aswan High Dam, Egypt (Photo: Douglas Dickens)

Fig.2   Kenana Sugar Scheme, Northern Sudan (Photo: New Civil Engineer)

In many other parts of the world where natural rainfall is sufficient to produce crops in most years, irrigation can be used to make up the failure of rainfall, or to lengthen the cultivation season. Here the need to irrigate is not so clear-cut. Potential increases in productivity have to be weighed against the extra time and labour required to meet this increased productivity. More intensive cultivation may endanger the fertility of the soil.

The Geography of Irrigation

Irrigation has been practised in some parts of the world for several thousands of years. Rice has been grown under irrigation in India and the Far East for nearly 5,000 years; the Nile Delta in Egypt, and the plains of the Tigris and Euphrates in Iraq were under irrigation 4,000 years ago. Figure 3 shows rice terraces 3,000 years old at Banani in the Philippines. Today over 200 million hectares of land are irrigated in five continents. This area increased from 117 million hectares in 1952, and is still growing. Table 1 gives figures for irrigated areas in the countries of the world in 1952 and 1972.

Fig.3 Three thousand year-old rice terraces at Bananue, the Philippines (Photo: Douglas Dickins)

These figures, at best, are estimates, and their accuracy varies with the way the statistics have been assembled. Sometimes they may be slightly over-estimated because authorities do not enjoy disclosing figures which show under-utilisation of investment. However they give a fair idea of the importance of irrigation in the agricultural economy of many countries, and demonstrate that practical experience in irrigation is widespread. South-East Asia takes the lead with nearly seventy per cent of the world total.

Table 1 — Irrigated areas of the world in 1952 and 1972

Data from International Commission for Irrigation and Drainage Annual Bulletins. Items marked * are the author's estimates.

Region and Country	Million Hectares 1952	Million Hectares 1972
1. SOUTH-EAST ASIA		
Burma	0.8	0.8
Ceylon	0.2	0.3
China	40.0*	74.0
India	19.7	32.7
Indonesia	1.8	3.8
Japan	2.8	3.4
Korea	0.4*	1.0
Malaysia	0.2*	0.3
Pakistan	12.1	12.0
Philippines	0.1	1.0
Taiwan	0.6	1.9
Thailand	0.6	1.9
Vietnam	0.1	0.2
Others	0.1*	0.1
	79.2	132.0
2. NORTH AMERICA		
Canada	0.2	0.6
United States	10.7	16.9
	10.9	17.5
3. EUROPE		
Albania	0	0.2
Bulgaria	0.2*	1.0
Czechoslovakia	0.03*	0.1
Denmark	0.02*	0.1
France	2.3	2.5

Region and Country	Million Hectares	
	1952	1972
Germany (Fed. Repub.)	0.1*	0.3
Greece	0.1*	0.7
Hungary	0.1*	0.4
Italy	2.2	3.2
Netherlands	0.05*	0.1
Poland	0.05*	0.1
Portugal	0.03	0.6
Rumania	0.05*	0.6
Spain	0.8*	2.3
United Kingdom	0	0.1
Yugoslavia	0.02*	0.6
Others	0.01*	0.1
	6.1	13.0

4. MIDDLE EAST

Afghanistan	0.6*	0.8
Iran	2.0*	3.1
Iraq	3.3	4.0
Israel	0.04	0.2
Saudi Arabia	0.02*	0.2
Syria	0.4*	0.5
Turkey	0.05	1.9
Others	0.1*	0.2
	6.5	10.9

5. U.S.S.R.

	6.0	10.4

6. AFRICA

Algeria	0.2	0.3
Egypt	2.5*	3.0
Libya	0.05*	0.2
Malagasy Republic	0.4*	0.9
Morocco	0.01	0.2
Senegal	0.05*	0.1
Somalia	0.05*	0.2
South Africa	0.4	0.6
Sudan	0.5	0.8
Tunisia	0*	0.1
Others	0*	0.2
	4.2	6.6

Region and Country	Million Hectares	
	1952	1972
7. CARIBBEAN AND CENTRAL AMERICA		
Cuba	0.3*	0.5
Dominican Republic	0.1*	0.2
Jamaica	0.04*	0.1
Mexico	1.7	4.0
Others	0.1	0.1
	2.2	4.9
8. SOUTH AMERICA		
Argentina	1.0	1.2
Brazil	0.05*	0.1
Chile	0.1*	1.3
Colombia	0	0.2
Ecuador	0.05*	0.1
Guyana	0.04*	0.2
Peru	0.05*	0.9
Venezuela	0.1*	0.4
Others	0.02	0.1
	1.4	4.5
9. AUSTRALASIA		
Australia	0.6	1.3
New Zealand	0.03	0.1
	0.6	1.4
WORLD TOTALS		
South-East Asia	79.2	132.0
North America	10.9	17.5
Europe	6.1	13.0
Middle East	6.5	10.9
U.S.S.R.	6.0	10.4
Africa	4.2	6.6
Caribbean and Central America	2.2	4.9
South America	1.4	4.5
Australasia	0.6	1.4
	117.1	201.2

Chapter 2
The Choice of Technology

There are many notable examples of heavy investments in large irrigation projects which have not turned out as planned and in which today less than fifty per cent of the irrigation facilities are actually being used. If large-scale planners and designers, with almost unlimited technical and scientific resources at their disposal, can make mistakes like these, it is understandable that it will often not be easy for the small-scale farmer to decide whether or not to introduce irrigation.

But because the output of major irrigation schemes is sometimes disappointingly low, more attention is now being given to the small-scale farmer and the scope for improving productivity in small units. The various physical factors, technical options and social and institutional influences which need to be considered are discussed in Chapter 3.

Fig.4 One of the irrigation canal headworks at the Nagarjunasagar Dam on the Kristna River, near Hyderabad, India, for the irrigation of 1½ million hectares (Photo: Douglas Dickins)

The Advent of Modern Irrigation

Many of the ancient irrigation systems which originated several thousand years ago in the East and Far East have continued without significant changes in their overall layout and methods of operation until the present time. Water supplies are still often unregulated and uncontrolled, and the distribution and amounts of water available for crops each year are precariously dependent on rainfall and run-off.

The first applications of modern engineering technology to irrigation were made in India during the nineteenth century, followed quickly by large-scale developments in the southern United States. During the first half of the twentieth century, traditional irrigation systems in many parts of the world were modified and improved. The most significant feature of these works was the development of the river dam or barrage (Figures 1 and 4) and large canal headworks which ensured a much more efficient and effective diversion of river waters, allowing water not required for irrigation to pass on down the river. Many of the well-known barrages in Pakistan, India, Egypt and Iraq were built during the first quarter of this century. At about the same time scientific engineering was being introduced into the already very extensive rice irrigation systems in Malaysia, Indonesia and other parts of the Far East (Figure 5).

Fig.5a Weir and canal headworks, Krasak River, Central Java, Indonesia

Fig.5b Regulating structure, Mataram Canal, Central Java, Indonesia

Usually, as modifications and improvements were applied to irrigation systems serving largely peasant agricultural communities, the government responsibility exercised through irrigation departments and services was confined to head works and major distribution, and little was done to carry those improvements down to field level where efficiencies were often very low. Irrigation efficiency is a measure of the effective use of the water supplied, and it is expressed as the ratio of the amount of water needed by the crops to the amount of water actually supplied. But even with low efficiencies most of these developments showed positive economic returns to the governments which were responsible for them, and at the same time did much to improve the food situation in rural areas. R.B. Buckley,* in a classic work on irrigation in India, wrote in 1919; "The beneficial results which both the security and increase of out-turn (i.e. crops) confer on the people are incomparably more valuable than the large revenue derived by the State".

Where private enterprise was also involved in irrigation development, rather more attention was devoted to improving efficiency at all levels including engineering improvements to minor distribution systems and field water applications. The 1920s and 1930s saw the expansion of the highly efficient

*Irrigation Pocket Book, E. & F.N. Spon, London, 1920.

sugar cane irrigation in Java, and the Gezira Irrigation Scheme for cotton, and other crops in the Sudan.

Changes in Attitude

Until the late 1960s, it had been generally assumed that the patterns of large-scale irrigation developed during the first half of the present century were universally beneficial. These assumptions were justified by results measured in terms of corporate production and corporate revenue, without looking too closely into the effective results at family and farm level. Furthermore, these results were achieved through the satisfactory functioning of large administrative and managerial units, which were sometimes government departments and sometimes commercial enterprises. In both cases they depended very much on loyal co-operation at all levels, and although occasionally this had to be enforced, by and large these orderly systems were accepted by all those working within them. By the early 1950s major political and social changes were beginning to stir in many parts of the developing world, and these changes have had a profound effect on all institutionalised activity. Irrigation schemes, which worked tolerably well in an earlier, more rigid social and economic system, now ran into all kinds of problems with staff and labour, maintenance and upkeep, and the effects of these changes were manifest in falling outputs and deteriorating performance.

By a curious anomaly the twenty years between 1950 and 1970 which saw so many disappointments in irrigation at field and farm level also saw an increase of seventy per cent in the areas of land under irrigation in developing countries, representing very substantial capital investments in new works. For many years irrigation planners and development authorities were not deterred by poor field results in their energetic promotion of irrigation projects. The problems of irrigation at the farm level have, however, been receiving some attention during the past decade. At a seminar sponsored by the United Nations Food and Agriculture Organization (FAO) in the Philippines in 1970 these problems were discussed. Among other things this seminar concluded that more attention should be given by governments to small-scale development.

More recently at its world congress in Moscow in 1975

the International Commission for Irrigation and Drainage appointed a committee on "assembling irrigation efficiency data", with a view to making recommendations for improving efficiencies at all levels, including field efficiencies.

Options for Development

There are many instances of large-scale irrigation schemes being under-utilised, and there are therefore very valid reasons for the collection of data which will lead to the better use of these existing facilities. But there is also a great need for a livelier response to the FAO Seminar recommendation that more attention should be given to small-scale development. The strongest argument in favour of small-scale irrigation is that it is easier than large-scale development because the human problems are reduced to a manageable scale. Certainly the sharing of a common source of water calls for co-operation between farmers, but experience seems to show that co-operative activities are more successful if they are not too large. If the development unit, in human terms, is small, then inevitably its resources for development will also be small. This will mean that construction work will have to be carried out at minimum cost, using simple methods, and local materials and labour wherever possible. This, in turn, will involve choosing the best available technology for the work in hand. Where equipment is installed, such as machinery for pumping, it should be of a kind which can easily be maintained and repaired by the skills which are locally available.

Chapter 3
Is It Worthwhile Irrigating?

A farmer contemplating irrigation will need to consider a number of factors. He will have to think about the climate, the soil, the availability of water, the crops to be grown and the amount of time and effort which he is prepared to put into the operation. Even in the simple practice of irrigation by watering can, most of these factors must be considered, if only briefly. Is it worth buying a can? Is it worth the effort of carrying the water? If the undertaking is likely to be more complex, involving the cost of developing or diverting a source of water, the purchase of equipment and materials and the employment of labour, then it will be more important to look carefully into the factors involved. To do this the farmer needs the best information he can get.

It is not always easy in remote areas to discover where the available information can be found or how to obtain it, but it is well worth a considerable amount of effort to find it. This may call for visits to the meteorological service, agricultural institutions, the water development authority (if it exists) and other organisations. If there is an agricultural extension service — and there are very few developing countries without this service — contact should be made with the nearest local officer who will usually be only too pleased to help a farmer interested in developing his resources.

Climate

The climate is a very important factor in any sort of cultivation. In places where there are fertile soils and conditions are favourable for irrigation but there is no rainfall, the need for irrigation is obvious. In other places where there is some rainfall, but it is insufficient in quantity or badly distributed in time, crops might be very much improved with irrigation. If rice is to be grown in paddies, then irrigation is a necessity. Whatever the circumstances it is important to obtain all possible information about the climate, the most useful data being rainfall, temperature, evaporation, humidity and the daily amounts of sunshine. Appendix B explains how these quantities are measured and recorded. As climatic conditions vary with the time of year, and irrigation may involve growing crops during months when there is no traditional cultivation, climatic conditions throughout the year need to be carefully studied. Because there are also variations from one year to another, records should be studied for as long a period as possible. Chapter 8 describes how this information is used in different climatic regions.

Soils

Most farmers understand soils, know where the better soils are to be found and how to use them for rain-fed cultivation. The introduction of irrigation can sometimes produce unexpected results if the farmer does not know a few scientific facts about his soils. A summary of the more important physical and chemical features of soil is given in Chapter 10.

The extra water of irrigation will bring about beneficial changes in most soils, increasing the amount of organic material (arising from extra cultivation), and, by keeping the soil wet, facilitating growth and the movement of nutrients from the soil into plant systems. But, the more water in the soil, the less air, and as air is also needed for the processes which maintain a soil's fertility, too much water can be harmful. Furthermore, some soils contain harmful soluble materials which irrigation water may bring up to the surface and subsequently precipitate (or release), seriously affecting the crops.

Every country has a department or section of soil studies, usually part of, or associated with its Ministry of Agriculture, and, largely through the help and encouragement of the Food and Agriculture Organisation of the United Nations, a large proportion of the agricultural land in the world has now been covered by soil survey maps. In many countries these maps show not only the distribution and types of soils, but also the land classified in accordance with its agricultural capabilities. These are all useful to the farmer and although he may not always be able to interpret them himself, there may be specialists in the agricultural service who can advise him on the basis of the mapped information, and he should seek this advice.

Topography

By topography we mean the form and shape of the land.

Almost any land, however steep, can be irrigated if it can be cultivated, depending upon the method of irrigation and the skill and resources of the farmer. But because it is important to control the water supply so that it will not be wasted, it is easier to irrigate by surface methods if the land is not steeply sloping. If basin irrigation is planned, each basin must be as level as possible. One of the advantages of overhead irrigation is that proper control of the water is not so dependent on the slope and shape of the land. But if water is to be supplied in pipes under pressure, it is necessary to know the height or 'head' for pumping. If water is to flow by gravity from one point to another, we must be certain that the starting point is higher than the delivery point.

All such information about heights and topography is obtained from topographical surveys and mapping. Existing maps, usually to a scale of 1 in 50,000 will give a general idea of the topography of an area, but this scale will be too small for irrigation planning. For a very small irrigation development it may be possible to judge heights by eye, but this will be rare, and some topographical survey work is usually essential. Appendix C gives some guidance on survey and mapping for irrigation.

Water

One of the commonest mistakes which people make when thinking about water for irrigation is to under-estimate the quantity which will be needed. In rural situations a good water supply for domestic and animal use (Figures 6 and 7) may be a very inadequate supply for irrigation. For example if all the water consumed in a month by a rural community of 1000 people with 250 cattle and 500 sheep and goats were used for irrigation, this would provide two irrigations a month to an area of about a quarter of a hectare.

The amount of water needed for irrigation depends not only on climatic conditions and the total area to be irrigated, but also on the crops to be grown. Tree crops and other *perennial* crops, which grow all the year round, need water throughout the year. *Seasonal* crops, which are cultivated from seed until they are harvested, need water only during the cultivation season. If irrigation water for seasonal crops is to be taken from a source which is liable to dry up during the dry season, the timing of the irrigation season will be an

Fig.6 Water supply installation, Um Isheishat, Western Sudan

Fig.7 Water supply yard, Um Isheishat, Western Sudan

important consideration. The water requirements of crops are discussed more fully in Chapter 9.

It is therefore important to know how much water will be needed for irrigation in terms of the crops to be grown and the area of land to be irrigated, and how much is available to meet this need. As the capacity of many sources such as springs or streams will vary very much with the season of the year and from one year to another, great care must be taken in assessing the 'safe' (never-likely-to-fail) supply. On this question the Government water development or water resources organisation should be consulted. They should know if there are any records of the flow of a spring or stream and where these records may be found. If no records are available, then the farmer himself should start measuring the source which he intends to use. Ways of doing this are suggested in Appendix D.

All natural surface waters and groundwaters contain some dissolved salts. In some places water may contain so much salt that it is unsuitable for irrigation. It is therefore wise to make sure that the water proposed for irrigation is not too saline (salty). The degree of salinity of water can be determined by laboratory tests, and if there is any doubt about the quality of the water to be used, professional advice should be sought.

Crops

Where irrigation is used to extend an existing cropping season, this often means cultivating a second crop at a time of the year when the climatic conditions are markedly different from the rain-fed cropping season. New crops have to be considered in the light of possible new conditions. Wheat, which can be grown under winter rain in Portugal or Cyprus will not thrive under irrigation in the summer because it is too hot. Paddy rice, accustomed to summer monsoon conditions, cannot be grown satisfactorily under irrigation in the cool dry winter in Pakistan or Northern India.

If a farmer intends to grow vegetables under irrigation for sale, he must be sure that his produce will sell. Some years ago a large dam was constructed in one country in S.E. Asia to enable the farmers to grow vegetables under irrigation during the dry season in addition to their traditional rain-fed rice during the monsoon. Little was done, either by the donor agency which provided the dam or by the government, to encourage the farmers to avail themselves of this new facility apart from a pilot project of a few hectares, on which some farmers were persuaded to grow irrigated cucumbers. At the end of the first irrigation season the farmers had several tons of cucumbers which they could not sell. The only possible market for this produce would have been in a city 500 km away, and the cost of the transport could not possibly have been recovered from sales.

Labour

Irrigation requires more labour than rain-fed cultivation. In addition to the activities associated with dry land farming, the irrigation water supply has to be managed and controlled. On large projects much, and sometimes all of the water control may be mechanised, but this will not be the case with most small farms where the farmer may have to manage his water source, look after his supply line, and distribute the water on his land.

With rain cultivation it is possible to leave the farm from time to time to participate in other non-farming activities, as no great harm comes to the crops. Under irrigation, water must be applied when it is due, and under harsh climatic conditions a day or two of delay in watering may result in serious crop losses. The farmer is therefore much more tied to his land when it is irrigated. Irrigated rice is particularly labour-intensive, and the dedicated commitment to cultivating successful paddy rice may not come easily to those not traditionally accustomed to this type of cultivation.

Legal Aspects

A number of countries now have legislation which governs the use of limited water resources, and it may be necessary for a farmer to obtain a licence to use a source of water. In countries where such legislation exists, the farmer should consult the responsible authority, which could be the Water Development or Water Resources Department, about his requirements. It may be that his needs are so small that they fall below the minimum for which licences are required, but it is as well to have the legal position clearly understood before embarking on a development.

There may be other legal aspects to be considered, such as common rights to a source of water, or access to land for the conveyance of water from the source to the field. Where several farmers share in the development of a source, this will call for some co-operative agreement over the management and use of the supply. Examples of how this is done in some countries are given in Appendix E.

Is it Worthwhile?

If having looked at all these rather daunting questions in a general way, the farmer decides to irrigate, he will then need to consider each one in more detail. His approach to the problems of planning for irrigation will depend on the geographical and climatic region in which he is situated, on his financial and technical resources and on the farming system that he intends to follow. Part II of this book describes the various methods of irrigation which can be practised and Part III looks at the problems of planning and design.

PART II
IRRIGATION PRACTICE

Chapter 4

Moisture Conservation Techniques

Run-off is the term given to that part of water from rainfall (and other forms of precipitation) which flows away from the land on which it has fallen. Where soils are impermeable and shallow and where land slopes are significant (say more than 5%), run-off occurs quickly, and only a little moisture remains in the soil. Under semi-arid conditions and high temperatures, direct evaporation from the soil quickly removes any moisture held in the surface layers and it may be impossible to grow crops. Various measures can be taken to reduce these soil moisture losses and to arrest run-off from the land so that crops can be grown.

Run-off Interception

Where surface water runs down a slope too quickly this can be retarded by creating level or nearly level ridges on the land to check the movement of the water, thereby enabling more water to be absorbed by the soil (Figure 8). Intercepting the run-off also helps to reduce the erosion of precious soil on steep slopes.

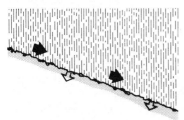 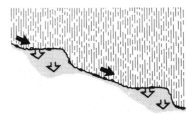

Fig.8 Run-off interception with ridges

The ridges may be made in various ways according to local soil conditions. If there are stones and gravel on the ground surface they can be collected to form the ridges. This method was practised by the Nabateans in the Negev Desert two thousand years ago and some of their constructions are still used for growing crops today. In the gently-sloping plain of the Gezira, Sudan, where stone and gravel are rarely found, ridges for intercepting run-off are made of the local clay soil. In steep, rocky terrain the ridges may take the form of terraces made of stones (Figure 9). Where land is ploughed in furrows, the furrows will intercept run-off if ploughed across the direction of the slope (Figure 10a).

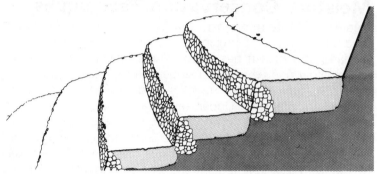

Fig.9 Run-off interception with terraces made of stones

 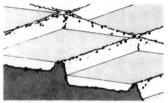

Fig.10a Furrows ploughed across the direction of slope   *Fig.10b Basins for intercepting run-off*

Where land is gently sloping or almost flat, run-off can be arrested by the construction of basins (Figure 10b). Most systems of embankments or terracing will have to cater for heavy storms or prolonged rainfall, and provision must be made for surplus water to move down the slopes into streams and drainage lines. In a few cases, with rock terraces and permeable soils, percolation through the terraces may be adequate, but usually it will be necessary to direct surplus water along the terraces or ridges into some prepared water-way such as a natural drainage line (Figure 11).

Run-off Farming

Run-off farming is the name given to the practice of concentrating surface run-off for cultivation in desert and semi-desert regions where there is never sustained stream flow. It is a technique which was used as long ago as 950 B.C.

Fig.11 Drainage of terraces

and recent investigations in the Negev Desert have revealed the remains of extensive ancient agricultural systems based on this method. Farms up to 3 ha in size in narrow valley bottoms were watered from catchment basins up to 60 ha in area on adjoining hill slopes. Run-off from the catchment basins was collected in channels and directed on to terraced fields. Modern experimental research has demonstrated that this system works successfully, and provided the proportions between catchment area and cultivated area are correct, cultivation can be supported where the total annual rainfall is less than 100 mm.

Contour Seepage Furrows

A system has been developed in Zambia for conserving run-off in seasonally water-logged areas near to rivers and streams, known as *dambos*. A *dambo* is a grass covered plain which slopes gently towards the river into which it drains and which collects run-off from adjacent higher ground. It has heavy hydromorphic soils which are waterlogged during the rains and which under natural conditions may remain water-logged for a considerable part of the following dry season. In this way *dambos* provide valuable grazing. As a result of increasing pressure on agricultural land leading to soil erosion and rapid run-off from catchment areas above the *dambo,* together with cultivation and over-grazing within the *dambo,* water passes through the area more rapidly and the land dries out more quickly. The natural storage in the *dambo* can be restored, and even improved, by the construction of contour seepage furrows. These are small ditches following contour levels across the *dambo* (Figure 12). These ditches, 15 cm deep, 45 cm wide at the bottom are best dug by hand, and the spoil placed on the down-slope side of the ditch to form low embankments. The ditches should be spaced so that there is a ditch line for every 0.40 m fall down the slope (i.e. every 20 m on a 2% slope, every 40 m on a 1% slope), and the spoil banks should be interrupted by a spillway opening every 25 to 30 m (Figure 13). These openings are necessary to allow free movement of storm water and avoid damage to the system. The 3.0 m wide spillway opening is improved by cutting a small drainage channel 5 cm deep down the centre of the spillway to carry small surplus run-off.

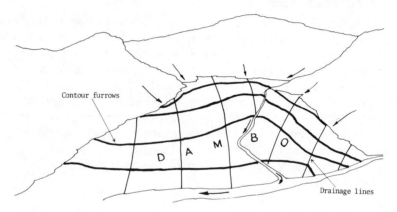

Fig.12 Contour seepage furrows

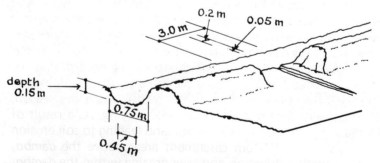

Fig.13 Details of seepage furrows and spillway

By increasing the capacity of the *dambo* for holding water, the contour seepage furrows will improve the quality of the natural vegetation, reduce the erosive effects of overgrazing, and, if so required, provide sub-soil water for seepage irrigation well into the dry season. If cultivation is to be undertaken where contour seepage furrows have been constructed, then cultivation plots will need to be protected from spill flow through the spillways by excavating drainage channels down the slope between the seepage furrows.

Mulching

The evaporation of moisture from soil can be reduced by *mulching,* a term describing the placing of material on the soil which suppresses evaporation and conserves water within the root zone. Mulching with a blanket of plant residues such as dead weeds, straw, hay or other waste products is practised traditionally in many parts of the world. Gravel in layers as thin as 5 to 10 millimetres can also be used.

Paper and polythene are now widely used as mulches. Latex (liquid rubber), asphalt and oil have all been used to establish vegetation in sandy desert situations, but a disadvantage of synthetic mulches is that they tend to be expensive.

Soil Moisture Trap

An inexpensive development of the mulching principle was evolved on a project in the Western Sudan in the mid-1960s. A very thin, and therefore cheap, plastic sheet, perforated with holes 2 mm diameter at 10 cm intervals was laid over sandy soil and covered with a 5 cm layer of soil. A ridge of soil was formed to enclose this prepared area (Figure 14).

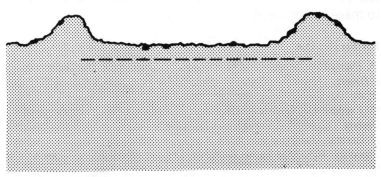

Fig.14 Soil Moisture Trap

Rain falling on the prepared area was absorbed by the soil surface and excess moisture passed through the holes in the membrane into the soil below. After the rain had stopped the blanket of soil above the membrane dried quickly, but moisture remained in the soil below for much longer. In this way, with successive showers of rain it was possible to build up a store of water in the soil, sufficient to bring plants to maturity, where under natural conditions this was not possible. Egg-plants, sown in seed beds and transplanted during the short wet season in July, were cultivated successfully, yielding fruit the following October, while those in an adjacent control plot without membrane storage failed for lack of water.

Humid Culture

Where water is scarce, plants can be grown in an enclosed system in which the water used is recycled. This process is known as *humid culture* and it has been demonstrated that crops and vegetables can be cultivated in this way both in the United Kingdom, and under more severe conditions in Saudi Arabia.

For this system the cultivation is enclosed in chambers, usually consisting of polythene sheeting supported on metal hoops to form semi-circular tunnel sections, which may be from 80 cm to 3 m in height. To prevent moisture escaping laterally through the soil, the edges of the polythene are buried to 15 or 20 cm, or attached to timber or concrete foundations. Air inlets are provided for ventilation, and the movement of air causes some moisture loss. Water is introduced initially by irrigating and it is found that plants will grow for many weeks before additional water is needed to make up for losses.

Further Reading

M. Evenari, L. Shanan and N.H. Tadmor, *The Negev: The Challenge of a Desert.* Harvard University Press, Cambridge, Massachusetts 02138, USA, 1971.
M. Evenari, U. Nessler, A. Rogel and O. Schenk, *Fields and Pastures in Deserts,* Eduard Roether, Buchdruckerei und Verlag, Darmstadt, W. Germany, 1976.
Doxiadis Associates and Doxiadis Ionides Associates, 'Agronomic Investigations in the 1964 Season', *Land and Water Use Survey in Kordofan Province of the Republic of the Sudan,* Document DOX-

SUD-A 35, UNDP/Food and Agriculture Organization, Via delle Terme di Caracalla, 00100 Rome, Italy, April 1965.
More Water for Arid Lands, National Academy of Sciences, Washington D.C., USA, 1974.

Chapter 5

Surface Irrigation

Surface irrigation systems are those which supply water to the land at ground surface level. They are also sometimes known as gravity systems because the water flows under the action of gravity and without the use of pumps. But because surface systems often include the use of pumps on main supplies, the term gravity is not appropriate to all surface systems. There are seven principal surface irrigation methods and these are *basin, border, furrow, corrugation, wild flooding, spate* and *trickle* irrigation.

Basin Irrigation

The basin method of irrigation is the most widely used, and easiest to operate. Most of the rice in the world is grown in basins, known in the East as paddies. Figure 15 shows paddy basins in the Philippines. Many other crops such as

Fig.15 Transplanting rice, Luzon Island, the Philippines
(Photo: Douglas Dickins)

cotton, grain, maize, groundnuts and vegetables are suited to basin irrigation, which can also be used in orchards, where each tree may have its own basin. The method involves dividing a field into small units, so that each has a nearly level surface. It is therefore most suited to flat land, but can be used on sloping land provided that the soil is deep enough to allow levelling without exposing the sub-soil. Small banks (levees, bunds, ridges or dykes) of earth 30 to 50 cm high are constructed round the area forming the basin, with inlet and outlet controls for water (Figure 16). The basins are filled with water to within about 10 cm of the top of the levees, and the water is retained until it infiltrates into the soil, or the excess is drained off. Basins may be of any size from one square metre to several hectares.

The main disadvantage of basin irrigation is that the levees interfere with the movement of animals and agricultural equipment used in land preparation and cultivation. Where the land is very flat there may be problems in draining off excess water from the basins, and this can cause delays and it also encourages the breeding of mosquitoes. Basin irrigation cannot be used for crops which are damaged by prolonged

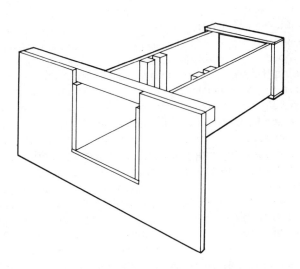

Fig.16 Small gated control structure for basin or border irrigation

standing in water; it may be used on most soil types, ranging from sandy soils to clay, but heavier soils are preferable because percolation losses are less.

The size of basins depends primarily on the rate of water supply available, the slope of the land and the texture of the soil. As one of the purposes of basin irrigation is to provide a uniform depth of ponded water over the whole area, the basin should be filled as quickly as possible. For a given rate of water supply basins in light sandy soils will therefore be smaller than basins in heavy clays. On flat land basins can be larger than on sloping land. Table 2 gives suggested basin sizes for various supply flows and soil types for relatively flat land.

Table 2 — Suitable areas for basins (sq metres)

Flow Litres/sec	Sand	Sandy Loam	Clay Loam	Clay
10	65	200	400	700
20	130	400	800	1,400
50	325	1,000	2,000	3,500
100	650	2,000	4,000	7,000

Water is distributed most evenly within a basin if the soil surface is level and variations between the highest and lowest levels in a basin should be less than 6 cm. Where the land is sloping, basins should be constructed in steps or terraces following the contours of the slope. The width of the basins between the steps will depend on the slope of the land and the amount of levelling which can be carried out without damaging the soil by the removal of too much top-soil. Where soils are shallow very little land levelling can be done, and terraces will be narrow. Normally the step or drop between terrace levels should not be more than 15 cm. Table 3 gives suggested spacing of contour steps for different land slopes, the wider spacing applying to soils where land levelling is permissible and the narrower spacing to soils where it is not.

The size of the basins on each terrace can be determined from Tables 2 and 3, as an example will illustrate. Suppose basins are to be formed on land with shallow sandy-loam soil sloping at 0.5%, and the available water supply is 20 litres/second. Assuming that the soil is too shallow to permit land levelling, the terrace spacing, from Table 3, would have to be 12 metres. A suitable area, from Table 2, would be

Table 3 — Suitable spacing of terrace steps for basins (metres)	
Land slope %	Spacing
0.1	150-60
0.2	75-30
0.5	30-12
1.0	15-6
1.5	10-4
2.0	7.5-3
3.0	5-2
4.0	3.75-1.5

400 sq.m., so the length of each basin should be 400/12 = 33.3 m.

The levees or embankments enclosing the basins should be formed by borrowing soil beside the embankments, and this can be incorporated with land levelling if this is needed. The banks should be constructed 0.75 to 1.0 m high, which after settlement would be 0.3 to 0.5 m high, with a base width 1.5 to 1.8 m and top width 15 cm to provide a pathway to the field.

Water can be supplied to the basins in two ways. It may be delivered to each basin from outlets on a supply channel, or it may be allowed to flow successively through a series of basins from a single channel outlet. For most crops, which do not need water continuously, the first method of water supply should be used. The second, continuous supply system is suitable for paddy rice cultivated under constant flooding, or for a single crop in several basins all requiring the same amount of water at the same time.

The time required to fill a basin can be calculated from the rate of flow of the supply, the area of the basin and the depth of water required to fill it. For example, if a basin 800 sq.m. in area is to be filled to a depth of 40 cm with a 20 l/s supply, the time required will be approximately:

$$\frac{0.4 \times 800 \times 1,000}{20 \times 3,600} = 4.4 \text{ hours}$$

This is the approximate time because we have not allowed for some of the water to be absorbed by the soil during filling. The amount of water absorbed by the soil will depend on the infiltration rate of the soil (see Chapter 11). For the basin areas and flow rates in Table 2, the time calculated as in the example should be increased by 10%, so that 4.4 hours should be corrected to 4.8 hours.

Border Irrigation

Border irrigation is suitable for large field units of 4 hectares or more. A field is divided by borders (low banks) into a series of strips which may be from 3 to 30 m wide, and from 100 to 800 m long, with an even, moderate slope along their length. Water is admitted at the top end of a strip and allowed to flow evenly across the full width of the strip and at nearly uniform depth. The rate of water application is adjusted so that the soil receives its correct amount of water as the sheet of water advances down the strip. When the water reaches the lower end of the strip, irrigation should be just about complete.

This system requires a relatively large flow of water, as a whole strip is covered with water during irrigation. It is best suited to deep, medium-textured soils with deep rooting crops. The land slope down the strip on fairly heavy soils should be not less than 0.2% to ensure water flow. Lighter soils, with their greater rates of infiltration, require steeper slopes, up to about 2%. Cross slopes should be eliminated wherever possible. This system is more appropriate to large scale than to small scale irrigation, and can be used for a variety of crops including grain, lucerne, pasture and orchards.

Border strips should be as long as possible without impairing water application efficiency. Long strips up to 800 m can be used on flat land with soils with very low infiltration rates. On soils with high infiltration rates, the length of strips may have to be 100 m or less. The length of strips also depends upon the flow rate of the irrigation supply. Too small a flow will not reach the end of a strip if it is too long. Table 4 gives a guide to the widths and lengths of border strips for different supply flows and soil types.

The levees or banks forming the borders to the strips should be 20 to 25 cm high after settlement and triangular in cross-section. Water is supplied to the top of a border from a supply channel through **outlets** or **turnouts**, which may be concrete or wooden gate structures (Figure 16), pipes placed in the channel bank with gate controls or portable syphons

Table 4 — Suitable dimensions for border strips					
	Soil Infil-		*Dimensions*		
	tration Rate,	*Slope*	*Width*	*Length*	*Flow*
Type	*mm/hr*	*%*	*m*	*m*	*litres/sec*
Sands	25 and over	0.2	15-30	60-90	220-450
		0.4	10-12	60-90	100-120
		0.8	5-10	75	30-70
Loams	7 to 25	0.2	15-30	250-300	70-140
		0.4	10-12	90-180	40-50
		0.8	5-10	90	12-25
Clays	2.5 to 7	0.2	15-30	350-800	45-90
		0.4	10-12	180-300	30-40

placed over the bank.

Furrow Irrigation

In the furrow method of irrigation, small channels (furrows) carry water down or across the slope of the land to wet the soil, and crops are grown on ridges between the furrows. The method is best suited to deep, moderately permeable soils with uniform, relatively flat slopes (preferably not steeper than 3%), and to crops which are cultivated in rows, such as vegetables, tomatoes, cotton, maize and potatoes. Furrow irrigation can be used in fields or plots of any size, and must be employed where surface irrigation is to be applied to crops which cannot tolerate standing in water.

In contrast to basin or border irrigation, furrow irrigation wets only part of the ground surface (between one fifth and one half). This reduces evaporation losses and the land dries out more quickly after irrigation. Uniform furrow irrigation requires considerable skill both in initial land grading and in controlling the water over local irregularities in land profile.

Furrows are usually V-shaped in cross-section, 25 to 30 cm wide at the top and 15 to 20 cm deep. Wider U-shaped furrows with a greater wetted area are sometimes used on soils which take water slowly. The spacing of furrows will depend on the crops to be grown, the space needed between rows for tillage and weeding and the lateral movement of water through the soil. The beds or ridges between the furrows may be flat or slightly rounded. Many crops are cultivated in rows 0.75 to 1.00 m apart, with one row on each ridge (Figure 17a). Vegetables are often planted with two rows 40 cm apart on each ridge (Figure 17b). Because water moves downwards through permeable soils more quickly than through impermeable soils, furrows should be closer together in more permeable soils.

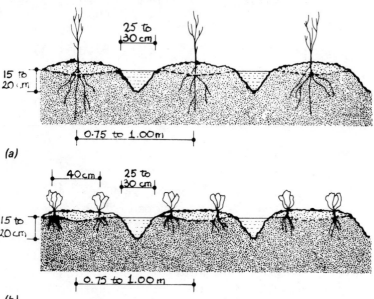

Fig.17 Irrigation furrows

For uniform irrigation, furrows should have a constant slope along their length. If this is not possible because of the topography, a slightly increasing slope is preferable to a decreasing slope. If the furrow slope is too steep, the velocity of the water will produce erosion, resulting in the formation of gullies and loss of soil. To avoid erosion the slope should not be more than 2% for most soils. Light sandy soils erode more easily than heavy clays. Where the natural land slope is more than 2%, the furrows should run at an angle to the line of greatest slope, and on steeply sloping land they may run almost along contours. The minimum practical slope for furrows is 0.1%, although flatter slopes are feasible.

The length of a furrow will depend on its slope and the texture of the soil. If the furrow slope is too flat and the soil is permeable, water may never reach the end of the furrow even if the water supply fills it at entry. If the slope is too steep the water will collect at the far end, and land at the head of the furrow will be short of water. For slopes up to about 1% in medium soils, furrows may be 300 to 400 metres long, but actual lengths have to be determined largely by trial and error in each situation. Table 5 gives suggested maximum furrow lengths for different soils, slopes, and water applications. The application depth is the total depth of water applied to a field in one irrigation (see Chapter 11).

Table 5 — Suggested maximum furrow lengths (metres)						
Furrow Slope %	Clays Application, mm.		Loams Application, mm.		Sands Application, mm.	
	200	300	100	200	75	125
0.05	400	400	270	400	90	190
0.1	450	500	340	470	120	220
0.2	510	620	370	530	190	300
0.3	570	800	400	600	220	400
0.5	540	750	370	530	190	300
1.0	450	600	300	470	150	250
1.5	400	500	280	400	120	220
2.0	320	400	250	340	90	190

Water is admitted to the head of each furrow, either one at a time or in groups, and the rate of flow is adjusted so that the furrow flows full but not overflowing, and so that soon after the water has reached the end of the furrow the required amount has seeped into the soil on each side of the furrow and beneath it, to satisfy the irrigation requirement (Figure 18). The rate of flow into a furrow depends primarily on the intake rate of the soil and the length of the furrow, and will be determined largely by experience in the field. Furrows in light sandy soil will accept water more rapidly than furrows, in clay soil. Table 6 gives infiltration rates for various soil textures and suitable furrow flow rates per 100 metre length of furrow, for furrows 1 metre apart.

For furrow spacing other than 1 metre, the inflow figures in Table 6 should be altered proportionately, the inflows being lower for closer spacing and higher for wider spacing. The figures obtained from the table should therefore be multiplied by the actual spacing. Thus if 0.6 l/s is the appropriate rate of flow for 1 metre spacing, the flow for 80 cm spacing should be 0.6 x 0.8 = 0.5 l/s.

Fig.18 Furrow irrigation at Mision La Paz (Photo: Mision de la Iglesia Anglicana, Argentina)

Table 6 — Soil infiltration rates and suitable furrow inflows per 100 metres of furrow length. Furrow spacing 1 metre.

Soil	Infiltration Rate mm/hour	Furrow Inflow l/sec/100 m length
Clay	1- 5	0.03-0.15
Clay-loam	5-10	0.15-0.3
Silt loam	10-20	0.3 - 0.5
Sandy loam	20-30	0.5 - 0.8
Sand	30-100	0.8 - 2.7

The time that water is allowed to flow into a furrow depends on the water application required. In practice this is often a matter for the farmer's judgement, but if the depth of application (D) and the rate of inflow into the furrow (Q) are known, the time of flow can be calculated from the formula:

$$T = \frac{D.S.L.}{3{,}600\ Q}\ \text{hours}$$

where D is in millimetres
S = spacing of furrows in metres
L = length of furrow in metres
Q is in litres/second.

If, for example, the soil is a sandy-loam, and an appropriate furrow inflow rate (Table 6) is 0.7 l/s per 100 m, the inflow to a furrow 285 m long should be 0.7 x 2.85 = 2 l/s. If the required application is 150 mm and the furrows are 80 cm apart, the time of watering for each furrow will be:

$$T = \frac{150 \times 0.8 \times 285}{3{,}600 \times 2}$$

$$= 4.75\ \text{hours}$$

If the available supply is 20 l/s, then this will water 20/2 = 10 furrows at the same time. The field area watered by a furrow is the length of the furrow multiplied by the spacing, or 285 x 0.8 = 228 sq.m. The area which can be watered at the same time is therefore 10 x 228 or 2,280 sq.m, and watering this area will take 4.75 hours. If the total area of the cultivation in the field is 285 m x 100 m, or 28,500 sq.m, the time needed to irrigate the whole field with a 20 l/s supply will be:

$$\frac{28{,}500}{2{,}280} \times 4.75 = 59.4\ \text{hours}$$

This is very nearly 60 hours, and if irrigation is carried out for 12 hours a day, it would take 5 days to water this field.

For annual crops such as grains and vegetables, furrows are constructed as part of the ploughing operations each year.

The field channels supplying the furrows may or may not be re-formed during ploughing, depending on the irrigation layout. On gentle uniformly sloping land with long furrow runs, the field channels are likely to be fairly permanent and undisturbed by ploughing and other activities. Where there are short furrow runs and therefore many field channels, it may be necessary to reconstruct the channels annually.

Outlets from the field channels to the furrows may be made in various ways. The most common practice is to cut openings in the field channel bank, at the same time blocking the channel with soil or a timber or metal check just downstream of the lowest furrow of a group to be irrigated. When the watering of one group of furrows is completed, the channel bank is repaired and the block in the channel moved to a new position upstream or downstream for the next group of furrows.

Although widely used, the practice of breaking field channel banks is not efficient because, unless the operators are very skilled it is not easy to ensure equal and uniform flow into the furrows. A popular and more efficient system is to use syphon pipes which carry the water over the channel bank. These may be made of aluminium, rigid plastic or synthetic rubber. To start a syphon flowing the whole pipe is immersed in the water in the field channel. Keeping one end under water the other end is blocked by placing a hand over it and the blocked end lifted over the channel bank and lowered until it is below the level of the water in the channel. When the hand is then taken away, the water will flow. For flexibility of operation it is better to use more than one syphon pipe for each furrow, so that adjustments to the flow can be made by adding or removing a pipe. The flow in a pipe can be reduced by raising the lower end to reduce the head.

The flow through a pipe depends upon its diameter, length and the head across it, which in the case of syphons is the difference between the water levels in the field channel and in the furrow when it is flowing. For short syphon pipes, the lengths of the pipes can be assumed constant, and flows taken as varying with the diameter and head. Table 7 gives syphon flows for different heads and pipe diameter.

Corrugation Irrigation

A variation of the furrow method is corrugation irrigation,

Table 7 — Syphon pipe flows (litres per second)				
		Head, cm		
Diameter of syphon. mm	5	10	15	20
10	0.05	0.07	0.08	0.09
20	0.19	0.26	0.32	0.73
30	0.42	0.59	0.73	0.84
40	0.75	1.06	1.29	1.49
50	1.17	1.65	2.02	2.33

in which close furrows about 10 cm deep are used without raised beds. The corrugations are spaced 40 to 75 cm apart, and during irrigation the whole soil surface is wetted. This method is used for close-growing crops which are not cultivated in rows, such as grain, pasture or lucerne.

As with normal furrow irrigation, the length of the corrugations depends on the slope of the land and the texture of the soil. This method can be used on steeper slopes than furrows and the corrugations are usually run down the greatest slope. Cross fall should be avoided if possible, and if unavoidable it should never exceed the slope of the corrugations. Corrugation irrigation is best suited to medium textured soils (silt loams or clay loams), in which water can move easily laterally through the soil. Table 8 gives suggested maximum length and spacing for corrugations for different slopes and for deep and shallow soils.

Table 8 — Length and spacing of corrugations						
		Clays		Loams		Sands	
	Slope	Length	Spacing	Length	Spacing	Length	Spacing
	%	m	m	m	m	m	m
Deep	2	180	0.75	130	0.75	70	0.60
Soils	4	120	0.65	90	0.75	45	0.55
	6	90	0.55	75	0.65	40	0.50
	8	85	0.55	60	0.55	30	0.45
	10	75	0.50	50	0.50	—	—
Shallow	2	120	0.60	90	0.60	45	0.45
Soils	4	85	0.55	60	0.55	30	0.45
	6	70	0.55	50	0.50	—	—
	8	60	0.50	45	0.45	—	—
	10	55	0.45	40	0.45	—	—

The rate at which water is admitted to the corrugations depends on the infiltration characteristics of the soil, and the length of the corrugations. Table 9 gives infiltration rates for different soil textures and suitable inflow rates per 100 metre length of corrugations spaced at 0.65 metres.

Table 9 — Soil infiltration rates and suitable corrugation inflows per 100 metres of corrugation length. Corrugation spacing 0.65 m.

Soil	Infiltration Rate mm/hour	Corrugation Inflow l/sec/100 m length
Clay	1-5	0.02-0.09
Clay-loam	5-10	0.09-0.2
Silt-loam	10-20	0.2 -0.4
Sandy-loam	20-30	0.4 -0.5
Sand	30-100	0.5 -1.9

For corrugation spacing other than 0.65 m the figures in Table 9 should be altered proportionately, the inflows being lower for closer spacing and higher for wider spacing.

Outlets from field channels to the corrugations are made in the same way as those for furrows (page 48), but because the corrugation system is used on steeply sloping land and the corrugation run is therefore short, a lot of land will be wasted by the space taken up by the field channels, and the channels will obstruct cultivation processes. This can be overcome by the use of *gated pipes,* which are portable pipelines with evenly spaced outlets for delivering water into corrugations. A gated pipeline can be laid across a field, at right angles to the corrugations without disturbing them, and the gates on the pipe adjusted to give the correct flow and run for the soil and land slope. The ends of the corrugation runs will simply be blocked off with soil. When irrigation in the first position is complete, the pipeline is moved to a second position down the field, and so on until the whole length of the field is watered.

As with all irrigation equipment, the use of gated pipes makes the operation more costly than using earth channels. Not only must the cost of the pipelines be considered, but also the cost of raising the water up to one metre to provide the necessary pressure in the pipeline. Professional advice should be sought in designing a gated pipe system.

Wild Flooding

Wild flooding, a term which originated in the USA, is a system used primarily for steep land with low-income crops where the uniformity of water distribution is not an important factor. Water is delivered at several points from a supply channel running along the upper edge of a sloping plot or field, and is allowed to move freely down the slope. It requires skill in the selection of points for releasing water, but otherwise is a simple system involving a minimum amount of land preparation and does not require much labour in operation. This method can be used for perennial forage crops which protect the soil from erosion. It is dangerous to use it on light erodible soils.

Spate Irrigation

The use of short flood spates from upland and mountainous areas to irrigate land in plains and lowlands where rainfall is insufficient for cultivation is known as spate irrigation. It is practised traditionally in many parts of the Middle East and notably in the south and east of the Arabian peninsular, in the Sudan on the borders of Ethiopia, and in Ethiopia.

It is, in effect, another form of the run-off farming described in Chapter 4. An annual rainfall which may vary between 50 and 300 mm falling on steep rocky catchments during a short rainy season produces short torrent floods in 'wadis' (water-courses which are normally dry) which can be diverted on to cultivable land with deep soil capable of absorbing large quantities of water in a relatively short time. Because the soils are deep their moisture capacity is great enough to support a crop on one or two good inundations.

The method is inevitably hazardous because the flood flows are quite uncontrolled and traditional earth and brush-wood diversions are easily carried away. Water-courses emerging from hills into plains have a habit of changing their courses every few years, and this can seriously affect diversion arrangements. The introduction of more permanent masonry or concrete diversion and headworks in recent years has helped to stabilise some of these systems. For irrigation on a small scale, and where the right conditions are found, there is much to be said for spate irrigation.

Trickle Irrigation

The application of water to the soil at a very low rate

(2 to 10 litres per hour) through small outlets (tricklers or emitters) is known as *trickle, drip* or *dribble* irrigation. Water is supplied to the tricklers through polythene pipes (12 to 16 mm diameter), laid along rows of crops so that the trickler discharges on to the soil in the immediate vicinity of the crop stems and roots. The water is supplied under low pressure (1 to 3 atmospheres), and the supply-line may include equipment for injecting fertilizer into the water supply. The small orifices (openings) of the tricklers are liable to clogging and therefore the water supply is filtered.

This system is expensive because of the equipment needed, and it is therefore limited to high-income market-garden crops. It is very economical in water use and highly suitable for light, controlled irrigation applications.

Further Reading

L.J. Booher, *Surface Irrigation,* Food and Agriculture Organization of the United Nations, Via delle Terme di Caracalla, 00100 Rome, Italy, 1974.

Ivan E. Houk, *Irrigation Engineering,* Vol. I, John Wiley and Son, New York, USA, 1951, Ch.16.

Josef D. Zimmerman, *Irrigation,* John Wiley and Son, New York, USA, 1966, pp.107-143.

Bruce Withers and Stanley Vipond, *Irrigation: Design and Practice,* B.T. Batsford Ltd, 4 Fitzhardinge Street, London W1H 0AH, 1974, pp.35-46.

FAO Irrigation and Drainage Paper 14, *Trickle Irrigation,* Food and Agriculture Organization of the United Nations, Via delle Terme di Caracalla, 00100, Rome, Italy, 1973.

Chapter 6
Sub-soil Irrigation

In many parts of the world conditions are favourable for the cultivation of crops by the application of water below ground surface. This method of sub-surface irrigation (also known as sub-irrigation) is practised widely on a small scale wherever there is low lying alluvial land adjacent to a river or stream and where the land and river bed are sufficiently permeable for a water table to be maintained in the ground at a suitable depth for plant growth. Where rivers and streams are uncontrolled, adjacent lands may be inundated at times of high flood, and if the flood period is followed by a long dry season, the water table in the adjacent lands will fall gradually, corresponding with the seasonal regression of the water source. The fall in river levels is usually much more rapid than the fall in groundwater level, which allows time for crops to be established and for their roots to pursue the receding water table.

In some countries in the Middle East and North Africa, in places such as along *wadi* (dry stream) beds or in coastal areas where a water table is not too deep, but out of reach of plant roots, a method is practised of digging holes over the water table and planting dates or vegetables in them.

Water Table Control

Measures to control river basins by means of dams or barrages, or to drain and reclaim low-lying and flooded land will affect the behaviour of water tables in these areas. A reservoir may create a permanent water table in peripheral alluvial land, fluctuating with the level of the reservoir itself, where previously the water table was seasonal or transient. Drainage and reclamation works may help to lower a natural water table during a wet season and, by controlling the drainage outflow in an ensuing dry season, these works may help to maintain groundwater at a level suitable for cultivation. This practice is common in many large alluvial plains.

By keeping water below ground level, it is used efficiently

and economically. Normal irrigation losses through open water evaporation are practically eliminated and deep percolation losses are controlled by the rate of drainage from the area. There is, however, a serious danger with this method. If either the water or the soils contain harmful salts, these salts may be brought to the surface of the ground by capillary action, and then it will be impossible to remove them except by heavy applications of water at the surface and a rapid lowering of the controlled water table so that the salts will be leached out.

Sub-soil Pipes

Attempts have been made to irrigate through perforated pipes buried in the soil. To be effective, as many pipes need to be laid in a field as there are furrows in furrow irrigation, and this makes the system extremely costly in equipment. If the pipes are to be out of danger of ploughing, they should be at least 40 cms below ground level, so heavy installation costs are added to the high equipment costs.

Pitcher Irrigation

A new technique, using ordinary baked porous earthen pitchers has been developed experimentally at Karnal, India. Pitchers of about 30 cm diameter were buried in pits (75 cm diameter, 60 cm deep) filled with manured soil, the tops of the pitchers being just above ground level. Pre-soaked seeds were sown around the pitchers, which were kept filled with good quality irrigation water, adding water daily as necessary. Gourds, pumpkins and melons were cultivated succesfully in this way.

A similar method has been practised experimentally in Iran using the Kuzeh, a clay jar with a narrow neck about 15 cm high and 8 cm in diameter. Several jars were buried in the ground and connected to a hose-pipe water supply by short lengths of plastic tubing. Plants were grown in the wetted soil round the jar, using both pure and saline water.

Further Reading

R.C. Mondal, 'Pitcher Farming'. *Appropriate Technology* Vol.1, No.3, Intermediate Technology Publications Ltd, 9 King Street, London WC2E 8HN, England, 1974, p.7 (reprinted from *World Crops,* March/April 1974).

'Kuzeh Pot Irrigation', *Irrinews,* No.11, Volcani Center, P.O. Box 49, Beit Dagan, Israel, 1978.

Chapter 7
Overhead Irrigation

Watering Can

The simplest piece of overhead irrigation equipment is the watering can (Figure 19), much used for small-scale gardening in temperate regions, but which is not so common in the developing countries in tropical or sub-tropical regions. Since all the water has to be carried by hand, the watering can method is limited to small plots with an easily accessible source of water.

Fig.19 Watering can

The size of plot which can be irrigated depends largely upon its distance from the source, and the time that it takes to fill the can at the source. One man with a plot adjacent to an easily accessible canal, river or shallow well could manage a plot of about 500 sq. metres. If he has to fetch his water from a point 100 metres away, he could only manage about half this area. All other overhead systems of irrigation require water under pressure. This pressure may be derived from an elevated source such as a tank or reservoir, or it may be produced by a pump.

Hose pipe

Wherever there is a piped water distribution system, it is possible to connect a hose pipe to a tap or outlet, and, provided there is sufficient pressure in the water as it emerges from the hose pipe, this can be used with a nozzle to throw water over a plot of land. For example, if water is available at a standpipe or tap at a pressure head of 20 m, then one man, using a 12.5 mm diameter hose pipe 200 m long and working continuously 9½ hours a day, could irrigate a plot of about 800 sq. metres. If his pipe were only 100 m long, then he could irrigate a plot of about 1200 sq. metres, because, with less friction, the shorter pipe will deliver more water in a working day.

A major disadvantage of this system is likely to be the cost of the water supply. An 800 sq. metre plot might require 160,000 litres in a six-month irrigation season. This quantity would be equivalent to six months of domestic water for 15 to 20 people in a rural area. Where piped water for domestic use is in short supply, it is very unlikely that it would be permissible to use it for irrigation. But there are places where piped water is available for irrigation and where the hose pipe can be used with advantage.

Sprinkler Systems

Of the various systems of irrigation the sprinkler method is the nearest to natural rainfall. Water, distributed under pressure through pipes, is discharged as a jet or spray into the air over the land to be irrigated. Because of its application efficiency, its adaptability to different types of terrain without the need for land levelling and because of its ease of operation, sprinkler irrigation is used extensively all over the world. However, it involves high initial costs for pumping machinery, piping and portable field equipment, and because supplying water under pressure uses a lot of energy, it is costly to operate. For a scheme drawing water from an existing river or canal, initial costs could be between US$1200 and $2000 per hectare. If the existing water source were at about ground level, annual costs for pumping energy and for the operation and maintenance of the system, excluding the farmer's time and labour could be between US$100 and $200 per hectare.

Sprinkler irrigation is best suited to medium and large farms of 10 hectares and above. It is also feasible to use sprinkler systems on small farms down to about half a hectare, but small units are relatively more expensive in initial cost (over US$2000 per hectare) and relatively less efficient in water use. Sprinkler irrigation is particularly adapted to light applications and therefore to coarse textured soils (sands and loamy sands) which have low moisture-holding capacities, because uniformity of distribution is not so dependent on the depth of application or on soil intake rates. Distribution is, however, liable to be distorted by the wind, so that areas with high prevailing winds are less suitable than areas with moderate winds.

Sprinkler irrigation pipework may be permanently buried below ground, partly permanent and partly portable, or fully portable in which all the pipework is laid on the ground and moved as required. Fully portable systems are most appropriate to small scale development.

For small scale intensive cultivation, nozzle lines (pipes with nozzles at regular intervals) may be used. These apply small quantities of water at low rates and are therefore suitable for nurseries and seed beds. Installation cost is high, and because the nozzles are very small, they are easily blocked and need frequent cleaning.

The most common type of sprinkler used with portable systems is the rotating head sprinkler, consisting of a head, with one or two nozzles, which is rotated slowly by the action of the water passing through it, and which waters a roughly circular piece of land round the sprinkler (Figure 20).

Fig.20 Typical sprinkler head (Photo: Wright Rain)

Rotating sprinklers operate under a wide range of pressures and discharges. For every operating pressure there is an optimum nozzle diameter to give the best dispersion of the water. Sprinklers are classified broadly into three groups according to their operating pressures, and these are given together with other characteristics in Table 10.

Table 10 — Typical rotating sprinkler characteristics

Characteristics	Low-Pressure	Medium-Pressure	High-Pressure
Operating pressure, atmospheres	1-2	2-5	5-10
Nozzle diameter, mm	1.5-6	6-20	20-40
Discharge, l/s	0.06-1	0.25-10	10-50
Diameter of coverage, m	6-35	25-80	80-140
Sprinkler spacing, m	9-18	18-54	54-100

High pressure systems involve high energy costs for pumping, and medium and low pressure systems are therefore more appropriate to the small scale operator. Low pressure systems are used for irrigating orchards and tree crops below the leaf canopy, for soils with high infiltration rates and for covering small areas. Medium pressure systems cover larger areas and are generally used for field crops. High pressure systems are used for high standing crops such as sugar cane. Giant sprinklers, consisting of a single high pressure nozzle operating at up to 10 atmospheres and covering a circle over 100 m in diameter, can be used for irrigating sugar cane and tree crops above the leaf canopy.

For very small plots, up to about 1000 sq. metres, a single small rotating sprinkler will be adequate. For larger areas, sprinklers are mounted, usually on 25 mm diameter standpipes, 1 to 2 m high, at equal intervals along the pipe which supplies them, so that the pipe-line with its sprinklers waters a strip of land. When this strip of land has received its quota of water, the pipe and sprinklers are then moved laterally to water a second strip of land adjacent to the first. In this way, a field unit can be watered by one or two sprinkler lines (Figure 21). The sprinkler line (or lateral) is made up of sections and all the equipment is provided with special joints and couplings so that it can be dismantled, moved and re-assembled quickly. The lateral pipe may be supplied directly from a portable pump for a small scheme, or from a hydrant on a buried pressure pipe system on a large scheme. The portable lateral line is well-suited to all crops which are cultivated in rows.

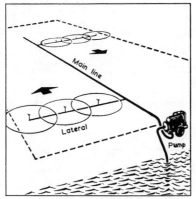

Fig.21 Simple sprinkler layout (Illustration: Wright Rain)

The circular area wetted by one rotating sprinkler depends upon its discharge and operating pressure. The precipitation rate over this area is not uniform, but by arranging the wetted patterns of sprinklers to overlap (Figure 21) reasonably uniform applications are achieved. The overlap is usually 50% or more of the diameter of the wetted area. Lateral pipe lines are made up of standard pipe lengths between 5 and 12 m, and the spacing of sprinklers along a lateral and the distances between lateral positions are in multiples of pipe lengths. Owing to friction losses along a lateral pipe, the discharge from each sprinkler on a lateral will fall progressively along the line. The number of sprinklers on a lateral, and therefore the length of the lateral, will be determined by the permissible drop in discharge between the first and last sprinklers. This drop should not be greater than 10% of the discharge of the first sprinkler. The length of the laterals may also be decided in relation to the shape and size of the fields.

A sprinkler irrigation system is designed to provide a calculated depth of water at a fixed rate of application. The application rate is determined from the intake characteristics of the soil. Water intake rates for overhead irrigation are given in Table 11. These rates are slightly lower than those for surface irrigation (Table 9) as there should be no ponding of water at the soil surface.

Table 11 — Water intake rates for overhead irrigation

Soil type	Intake rate mm/hour
Clay	1-5
Clay-loam	6-8
Silt-loam	7-10
Sandy loam	8-12
Sand	10-25

The amount of water which reaches the soil root zone is less than the discharge of the sprinklers because of losses by evaporation and wind in the air, by evaporation from wet foliage and wet soil, and by deep percolation in the soil. The ratio of the effective water application to the total application from the sprinklers, is known as the *application efficiency*, and this is usually from 70% to 80%.

The required depth of application is calculated from the soil characteristics, as described in Chapter 11, and the frequency of irrigation from the crop water requirements as described in Chapter 9.

There is a wide choice of sprinkler equipment available and there are many possible combinations of sprinkler spacing, nozzle discharge, and operating pressure to give the required watering performance. It may therefore be necessary to seek professional advice in choosing the appropriate equipment and designing a sprinkler layout. The following example illustrates how a simple scheme might be designed.

A farmer proposes to use sprinkler irrigation on a piece of land 160 m x 120 m adjacent to a river from which he can pump water (Figure 22). For the crops which he intends to grow, a medium pressure system will be suitable, and from a study of the climatic and soil conditions he has found that he will need a maximum application depth of 60 mm every 10 days. The maximum intake rate of the soil is 8.5 mm/h, and with an application efficiency of 80%, the gross application would be 75 mm, at a maximum rate of 10.6 mm/h.

Because there are many different types of sprinkler irrigation equipment available, each with a range of sprinklers with different specifications and characteristics, there may be several systems and layouts which will adequately meet the farmer's requirements. In this example we consider two

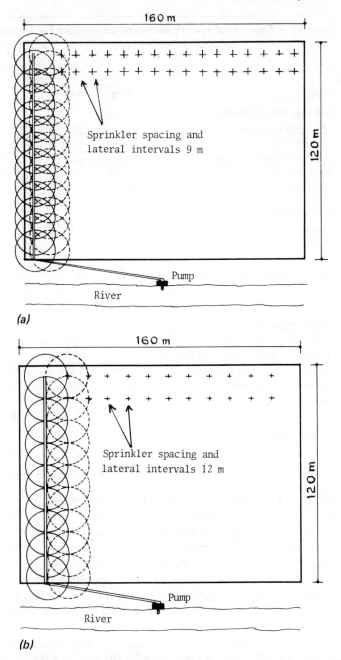

Fig.22 *Possible arrangements for a small sprinkler irrigation system*

Table 12 — Example of specifications and calculations for a small sprinkler irrigation system

Details	Units	Possible arrangements (a)	(b)
Sprinkler specifications			
Operating pressure	atm	2	3
Nozzle diameter	mm	4	4.5
Discharge per sprinkler (q)	l/s	0.25	0.37
Spacing (s)	m	9 x 9	12 x 12
Application rate (r)	mm/h	10.4	9.5
Field details			
Number of sprinklers on lateral $n = \dfrac{120}{s}$	no	13	10
Number of lateral positions $p = \dfrac{160}{s}$	no	18	13
Application time, to apply 75 mm gross, t = 75/r	h	7.2	7.9
Add time for moving equipment	h	0.7	0.7
Total time for one position	h	7.9	8.6
Time for 2 positions per day	h	15.8	17.2
Number of days required for complete irrigation, $\dfrac{p}{2}$	days	9	6.5
Pump supply required Q = q.n.	l/s	3.25	3.70

possibilities, the details of which are given in Table 12.

Of the two possibilities (a) may cost a little more in equipment, needing 13 sprinklers and risers instead of 10. But in other respects it appears to be the better arrangement. The lower operating pressure and lower discharge mean less energy for pumping and therefore lower operating costs.

Regarding the time programme, (a) fits a 10-day cycle better than (b). On the other hand a farmer may prefer a slightly faster cycle (6½ days instead of 9 days) if it gives him more time for other activities. If he is prepared to irrigation for 24 hours a day, scheme (a) would take 6 days and scheme (b) just over 4½ days.

It will be clear that many factors need to be considered in selecting equipment and planning a sprinkler irrigation system, and it may therefore be prudent to seek professional advice on these matters.

Further Reading

Arthur F. Pillsbury, *Sprinkler Irrigation,* Food and Agriculture Organizattion of the United Nations, Via delle Terme di Caracalla, 00100 Rome, Italy, 1968.
Josef D. Zimmerman, *Irrigation,* John Wiley and Son, New York, USA, 1966, Ch.9.
Bruce Withers and Stanley Vipond, *Irrigation: Design and Practice,* B.T. Batsford Ltd, 4 Fitzhardinge Street, London W1H 0AH, England, 1974, pp.47-54.

PART III
PLANNING AND DESIGN

Chapter 8
Climatic Factors

The importance of information about the climate when planning for irrigation has been mentioned in Chapter 3, and Appendix B explains how the most important climatic factors, rainfall, temperature, evaporation, humidity and sunshine are measured.* In this chapter we describe how this information can be used.

Most of the countries where irrigation is needed fall into one of three principal climatic regions: *mediterranean, monsoon* and *wet tropical.* The climatic characteristics of each of these regions are different, and farmers will view their irrigation possibilities in different ways accordingly.

Mediterranean Regions

The Mediterranean Regions take their name from the conditions common to the countries bordering the Mediterranean Sea, and include not only Mediterranean countries but also other parts of the Middle East, the Black Sea area, the west coast of the United States, the coastal belt of Chile, the southern tip of South Africa and parts of South and Western Australia. For the purpose of this section semi-arid regions which have seasonal conditions similar to the Mediterranean regions (but drier) have also been included. Examples of these are central Arabia, Iraq and parts of the western United States. In all these regions most of the rain falls in the cool winter months and the summers are dry and warm or hot. Where winter rainfall is usually adequate, rain-fed crops are grown in the winter; irrigation may be needed either to supplement a shortage of rainfall for the winter crops, or to extend cropping into the summer months. When irrigation is needed in the winter it is clearly important to know something about the patterns of rainfall in order to plan irrigation requirements. If irrigation in the summer months is contemplated, information will be needed about

---

*Wind is also an important climatic factor, but its measurement is not yet extensive enough in many countries to be of general practical value.

significant rainfall at the beginning and end of the summer and about the length of the summer period.

If the farmer is planning to irrigate during the summer months he will almost certainly know from experience which these months are. But rainfall records will be useful in planning his cropping seasons, and also in assessing the capacity of his source of water for irrigation if he is proposing to use a small local source such as a spring or stream. If the farmer has no previous experience of growing crops under irrigation in the summer, then a study of records of temperature and humidity during the summer months would help him to choose the most suitable varieties for the hot season.

Monsoon Regions

The Monsoon Regions lie in the tropics and sub-tropics, and they are characterised by a dry, and sometimes very dry winter and usually a well-defined wet season in the summer. These regions include the densely populated countries of the Indian sub-continent and south-east Asia, much of central and tropical South America and of northern Australia. The natural time for cultivation is with the summer rain, and irrigation may be needed either to supplement rain when it is deficient, or to enable crops to be grown in the dry winter months.

Information about climatic conditions will assist the farmer just as for the Mediterranean regions, except that the seasonal conditions are reversed. Temperature and humidity will be particularly significant if consideration is being given to irrigating in winter crops or vegetables which are traditionally grown in the humid summer months.

The Monsoon Regions include many of the main rice growing areas of the world in South-East Asia where irrigation has been practised for hundreds of years. As paddy rice is grown under flood irrigation, rainfall tends to supplement the irrigation; rainfall records will indicate the proportion of total water requirements which may be expected from natural rainfall, and will thus contribute to the economical use of irrigation water. If the quantity of rain falling in a heavy storm is measured, then the irrigation supply should be reduced by an equivalent amount. In practice this may not be easy to achieve in an open channel supply because of the time lag between reducing the supply at source and the reduction being felt at the field.

Wet Tropical Regions

Although the Wet Tropical Regions, which lie on or near the equator and at low altitudes, have high rainfall which occurs for most of the time, they do have dry periods in the year. As temperatures are always high, soil moisture can be quickly exhausted during these dry periods, so that there is a need for irrigation. These regions include West Africa and the Congo Basin, and equatorial parts of south-east Asia and South America.

With no clearly defined winter and summer, climatically suitable crops can be grown at any time of the year in these regions, provided that moisture is available in the soil throughout the growing season, and provided that there is adequate sunshine for maturing and ripening. Often in these regions annual rainfall patterns are bi-modal, which means that there are two identifiable wet seasons each year, alternating with dry periods. Under such conditions it is very useful to study rainfall and other climatic information so that irrigation cropping patterns can be planned to make the best of the climate.

Sometimes sunshine for ripening may be the governing factor which determines the harvesting and consequently the planting dates for a particular crop. Suppose, for example, the best sunshine period occurs after the second rains and that the crop is planted during the first rains. If the total rainfall in the two seasons is insufficient to meet the crop's requirements, irrigation will be needed as a supplement to rainfall, particularly at the critical time of planting, and also during the dry interval between the two wet seasons.

The Use of Rainfall Records

Because rainfall varies from year to year in total amounts and in its timing and pattern each year, it is necessary to measure rainfall as accurately as possible for a number of years. The length of the record needed is discussed in Chapter 15. A minimum of five years is usually considered essential, but even records for one complete year are better than nothing. In places were the average rainfall in the wet season is less than 500 mm, the amounts of rain each year are very variable. Short term records may therefore be unreliable. For example, suppose records of annual rainfall for five years gave the following results:

Year	1	2	3	4	5	Average
mm	440	580	290	310	380	400

To the farmer planning to irrigate the low rainfall years are important, in this case years 3 and 4. If he had only measured rainfall in years 1 and 2, he would have little idea of what was going to happen in year 3. Hence 5 years' records are better than 2 or 3. But because climate shows trends, with successions of wet years and successions of dry years, records for longer than 5 years should be obtained if available.

In this example, the farmer may have found that during the five years of records he got his best crops in years 1 and 5, and that in the wettest year, 2, results were poor because the wet season lasted for too long, and this damaged the ripening crop so that he had a bad harvest. These observations would tell him that the amount of water needed for a good crop would be equivalent to the rainfall in years 1 and 5, and the average amount for these two years was 410 mm. If 410 mm is taken as the seasonal crop water requirement, then in year 3, the driest year, with 290 mm of rainfall, the difference between 410 and 290, which is 120 mm, will give the amount of extra water to be provided by irrigation in year 3. In year 4, 410-310 = 100 mm of irrigation would have been needed.

While it is important to know the total amounts of irrigation water required in a season, it is even more important to know the maximum amount of water to be provided in one watering. At the height of the irrigation season this maximum amount of water will have to be provided in a given time, and this determines the *capacity* of the system, or the rate of flow which the system must be designed to deliver.

Rainfall is measured daily, and daily amounts are added up to give monthly and annual figures. A study of daily and monthly records will show the length and frequency of dry periods when irrigation will be needed, and this information, in conjunction with temperature and evaporation figures will enable the maximum irrigation requirements to be determined, on the basis of crop water requirements, as explained in the next chapter.

Chapter 9
Crops and Water

Plants need soil, sunlight, air and water to enable them to live and grow. Water is an essential component of all plant tissue and fulfils three primary functions. It keeps plants erect by filling the cells which make up plant tissue; it acts as a cooling agent in evaporating from the leaves, preventing overheating under hot conditions; and it carries nutrients in solution from the soil into the plants through their roots. The growth of plant material is produced from the combination, with the aid of sunlight, of a gas in the air, (carbon dioxide), with water and nutrients from the soil.

Evaporation Processes and Consumptive Use

Evaporation is the process by which water, in the form of water vapour, enters the atmosphere from open water surfaces such as the sea, lakes, ponds, rivers, or from wet land surfaces. *Transpiration* is the evaporation which takes place at the surfaces of plant leaves, described above. *Evapotranspiration* is the total movement of water vapour into the air from land which supports plant life. It includes transpiration from the plants, evaporation from damp soil and evaporation from any open water that may be present in furrows or depressions following irrigation or heavy rainfall.

The amount of water used in evapotranspiration is the quantity which is important for irrigation planning, because in the absence of rainfall, irrigation has to provide this water. Evapotranspiration varies with climatic conditions in the same way as open water evaporation. When the climate is hot and dry, the rate of evapotranspiration is high; when it is cool or humid the rate is low. When there is a wind it is higher than when the air is still. Evapotranspiration, like rainfall and evaporation is expressed in terms of depth of water (millimetres), and the rate of evapotranspiration in millimetres per hour. In regions where there are marked seasonal changes in climate there will be corresponding changes in the rate of evapotranspiration; where there is little seasonal climatic change, the rate will be much the same throughout the year.

Under natural conditions without irrigation, the actual evapotranspiration which takes place from land supporting vegetation at the end of a hot dry season will be very low because the soil is quite dry and there is therefore no available moisture. The term *potential evapotranspiration* is used to describe the evapotranspiration which could occur under these conditions, if water were freely available to the plants, which is what irrigation would provide.

Consumptive use is a term which originated in the United States and describes the quantities of water used by land supporting vegetation and crops. It is therefore the same quantity as evapotranspiration, and is also expressed in depths of water.

It is not easy to measure evapotranspiration accurately, but it can be estimated from measured climatic data.* For this purpose a quantity known as the *reference crop evapotranspiration* is used, defined as "the rate of evapotranspiration from an extensive surface of 8 to 15 cm tall green grass cover of uniform height, actively growing, completely shading the ground and not short of water". It is given the symbol ET_o and can be calculated in a number of ways, one of which will now be described.

Calculating ETo from Pan Evaporation

The measurement of evaporation by pans is described in Appendix B. Pan evaporation (E_{pan}) can be converted to ET_o by multiplying it by a pan coefficient, K_p. The value of this coefficient differs for different types of pan, and for the same type of pan it varies with the relative humidity of the air and the speed of the wind at the time of measurement, and with the siting of the pan in relation to crops and vegetation. Table 13 may be used as a guide to selecting the appropriate value for K_p with American Class A type evaporation pans.

Crop Water Requirements

Under the same climatic conditions, different crops require different amounts of water, and the quantities of water used by a particular crop vary with its stage of growth. Initially during seeding, sprouting and early growth, a crop uses water at a relatively slow rate. As growth develops this

---

*It can also be estimated by measuring changes in soil water content.

Table 13 — Pan Coefficients (Kp) for American Class A type evaporation pans

Relative Humidity	Cropped Area			Dry-Fallow Area		
	Less than 40%	40%- 70%	Over 70%	Less than 40%	40%- 70%	Over 70%
Wind:						
Light	0.65	0.75	0.85	0.60	0.70	0.80
Moderate	0.60	0.70	0.75	0.55	0.65	0.70
Strong	0.55	0.60	0.70	0.50	0.55	0.65
Very Strong	0.50	0.55	0.60	0.40	0.50	0.55

rate will increase, reaching a maximum in most crops at the approach of flowering and then declining towards maturity.

The actual amount of water used by a crop, or *crop evapotranspiration (ETcr)* is related to reference crop evapotranspiration (ETo) by a crop coefficient Kc, so that ETcr = Kc.ETo. The coefficient Kc may vary from 0.3 to 0.35 during initial growth to over 1.0 at mid-growth, and then falling below 1.0. For irrigation system designs, the maximum crop water requirements are the significant quantities needed. Figure 23 shows a typical crop coefficient curve. Stages of growth are shown as percentages of the total growing period, and this curve indicates how Kc changes with growth for most crops. There are, however, differences

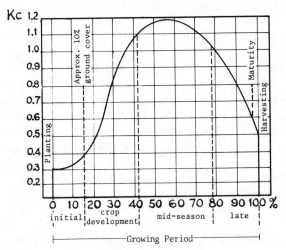

Fig.23 Typical crop coefficient curve

between crops, and Table 14 gives crop coefficients for a selection of crops at mid season and at final growth, under both humid and arid conditions, and the ranges of their growing periods. Generally growing periods are shorter in warm climates with long hours of sunshine, and longer in cool climates.

Table 14 — Crop Coefficients (Kc) for various crops and their growing periods

Crop	Relative Humidity more than 70% (humid)		Relative Humidity less than 20% (arid)		Growing Period Days
	Mid-Season	Final Growth	Mid-Season	Final Growth	
Barley, Wheat	1.1	0.25	1.2	0.2	120-165
Green Beans	0.95	0.85	1.0	0.9	75-90
Maize	1.1	0.55	1.2	0.6	80-110
Millet	1.05	0.3	1.15	0.25	105-140
Sorghum	1.05	0.5	1.15	0.55	120-130
Cotton	1.1	0.65	1.2	0.65	180-195
Tomatoes	1.1	0.6	1.2	0.65	135-180
Cabbage Cauliflower	1.0	0.85	1.1	0.95	80-95

Net Irrigation Requirements

A farmer planning irrigation must consider all aspects of crop water requirements including the growing period variations, his cultivation programme for each crop, and any possible contribution from rainfall. This can be illustrated by an example taken from a proposed development in Uganda. One of the crops to be grown was cotton, and a variety which required water for 5½ months. Two cropping patterns were possible which would allow for picking during the relatively dry weather between October and March: an early crop from May to October or a later crop from August to January. Net irrigation requirements (In) for the cotton were calculated from climatic data, and the results are shown in Table 15. The table shows the effective rainfall (Rd) and reference crop evapotranspiration (ETo) in monthly amounts for a year. As would be expected, evaporation (and consequently evapotranspiration) are high when the rainfall is low. Effective rainfall was taken as the '20%-dry' monthly rainfall, which means that amount of of rainfall in a particular month which is not exceeded for 20% of the total number of years of records. Thus the '20% dry' rainfall for March at 66 mm means that in say 30 years of rainfall records for March, the amounts for March for 20% of the years (i.e. 6 years) were 66 mm or less.

Table 15 — An example calculation for net irrigation water requirements for cotton in Uganda

All water quantities are in millimetres.

Rd = effective rainfall, ETo = reference crop evapotranspiration, Kc = Crop coefficient, ETcr = Crop evapotranspiration, In = net irrigation requirement.

Month	Rd	Eto	Early Crop Kc	ETcr	In	Late Crop Kc	ETcr	In
March	66	171						
April	196	159						
May	170	161	0.35	56	0			
June	94	153	0.65	99	5			
July	122	158	1.05	161	39			
August	137	158	1.20	190	53	0.35	55	0
Sept.	104	156	1.05	164	60	0.65	101	0
Oct.	91	161	0.65	105	14	1.05	169	78
Nov.	61	159				1.20	191	130
Dec.	38	164				1.05	172	134
Jan.	18	171				0.65	111	93
Feb.	38	157						
Totals	1,135	1,928		775	171		799	435

Several interesting facts emerge from this table. Because rates of evapotranspiration are much the same throughout the year in Uganda, the total amounts for ETcr and the peak monthly values are similar for the two crops. But the irrigation requirements are very different, due to the rainfall pattern, so that the second crop would need two and a half times as much irrigation water as that for the first crop. Also the maximum irrigation requirement for the second crop (134 mm in December) is more than twice as much as that for the first crop (60 mm in September), so that the second crop would need a correspondingly greater irrigation system capacity.

Irrigation Efficiency

The amount of water (If) delivered to the field in which crops are growing is greater than the net crop irrigation requirement (In) owing to the field application losses. With surface irrigation these losses arise from deep percolation in free draining soils, and from overspill and wastage of water. With overhead irrigation the field losses occur primarily through the direct evaporation of water in the air before reaching the crop and from the effects of wind distorting the spray pattern. The ratio In/If is known as the field *irrigation efficiency,* which may be expressed either as a factor or as a percentage. Table 16 gives field irrigation efficiencies appropriate to different types of irrigation.

Table 16 — Field irrigation efficiencies for different methods of irrigation	
Irrigation Method	*Efficiency*
Surface	
Basin (except rice), border, furrow, corrugation	0.4-0.6
Flooded rice	0.3
Overhead Sprinkler	0.6-0.8

In the example given in Table 15 the net irrigation requirement (In) for the early crop in the month of maximum demand (September) is 60 mm. If the field efficiency for surface irrigation here is taken as 0.5 then the field irrigation requirement for the month would be 60/0.5 = 120 mm. If sprinkler irrigation is used with an application efficiency of 0.7 the sprinkler application required for the month would be 60/0.7 = 86 mm.

Where irrigation water is supplied to a field by open channel, losses occur in the channel from evaporation and, in the case of earth channels, from seepage through the sides and bed of the channel. Suitable factors for these conveyance losses to give overall irrigation efficiencies are given in Chapter 14.

Water Quality

In general physical impurities such as sediment and silt in suspension in irrigation water are not harmful to agriculture and may help to maintain the fertility of the soil. Chemical impurities dissolved in the water can be harmful when present above certain fairly well-defined limits.

All natural waters contain some impurities. Rainfall picks up traces of gasses such as carbon dioxide from the air. Surface run-off dissolves small quantities of materials on the land surface and groundwater sometimes contains quite high concentrations of salts. The principal salt constituents that may be present in irrigation water are chlorides, sulphates and the element sodium. Particular salts are not necessarily harmful, but the total concentration of salts above a particular limit may be harmful. Common salt (sodium chloride) is one of the most widespread impurities in water. It accounts for four-fifths of the dissolved salts in sea water.

The quantity of salt in a sample of water can be determined by boiling the sample dry and weighing the solid residue which is left, and this gives the *Total Dissolved Solids (TDS),* expressed in parts per million (ppm) by weight equivalent to milligrams per litre (mg/l). Salinity is also indicated by the electrical conductivity of a solution, expressed in micromhos per cm, conductivity increasing with salinity. Because even very small traces of boron can be harmful to crops, the boron concentration in parts per million is also used as an indicator of the quality of irrigation water. Standards for irrigation water in terms of these various quantities are given in Table 17.

Table 17 — Standards for irrigation water				
TDS = total dissolved solids				
Quality of water	*Crops suited*	*Conductivity micromhos/cm*	*TDS mg/l*	*Boron ppm*
Good	All crops	50-500	0-600	0-0.5
Moderate	Injurious to sensitive crops	500-2200	600-2000	0.5-2
Poor to unsuitable	Harmful to most crops	over 2200	over 2000	over 2

The actual concentration of salts which is harmful in any particular situation depends very much on the chemical characteristics of the soil and on the type of crops being grown. Under favourable conditions where soil has a low clay content it may be possible to cultivate under irrigation with highly saline water up to 5,000 mg/l. The different levels of salt tolerance of various crops are shown in Table 18.

Table 18 — Relative tolerance of crops to salinity		
High tolerance	*Medium tolerance*	*Low tolerance*
Barley	Alfalfa	Citrus
Cotton	Cantaloup	Clovers
Date palm	Figs	Field beans
Grasses	Grapes	Green Beans
Rape	Maize	Soft fruits
Spinach	Oats	
	Olives	
	Peppers	
	Potatoes	
	Rice	
	Rye	
	Sorghum, Wheat, Vegetables	

Further Reading

FAO Irrigation and Drainage Paper 24, *Crop Water Requirements,* Food and Agriculture Organisation of the United Nations, Via delle Terme di Caracalla, 00100 Rome, Italy, 1977.

Chapter 10
Physical and Chemical Characteristics of Soil

Soil has aptly been defined as the material in which plants grow. It is, therefore, any earth material which contains air, water and plant food in a state in which plants can use them. A fertile soil is a soil in which plants grow well, and fertility is maintained by replenishing the soil with the requirements for plant growth.

Soil Formation

Soil material is formed from the breaking-down of rock into small particles by a process known as *weathering.* Weathering occurs under the influence of rain, snow, ice, air, wind, temperature change and the chemical action of slightly acid water containing carbon dioxide from the air. The weathering rock, from which soils are formed, is known as the parent material. The chemical and physical properties of its parent material play an important part in determining the characteristics of a soil.

If the weathering rock is on a slope, the particles produced will be washed down by rainwater until they reach level ground or some obstacle which prevents further movement, when they will settle and accumulate to form the basic ingredients of soil. In exposed places wind also plays its part in the transport of weathered particles. Soil is also formed in some cases directly over its parent rock without lateral particle movement.

In time seeds, carried by the wind, in bird droppings or by surface water, will arrive and germinate. The development of plant life and the recycling of plant nutrients through the decomposition of vegetable material completes the formation of a fertile soil.

The Composition of Soil

A fertile soil contains two distinct solid components: mineral and organic matter. The organic matter usually amounts to one hundredth to one-tenth by weight of the mineral materials, except in the case of peat, in which the solid matter is nearly all organic. The process of decomposition of vegetable matter at the soil surface produces a material known as *humus,* which gives top-soil its usually dark colour.

As every farmer knows, the appearance and composition of most soils varies with depth below the ground surface, and often distinct layers or *horizons* can be identified. While most of the agricultural activity takes place in the top-soil or upper layers, the composition of the sub-soil or lower layers plays an important part in determing the drainage characteristics of a soil. A sandy or gravelly sub-soil provides good drainage; a heavy clay sub-soil, poor drainage.

Under arid and semi-arid conditions soils with impervious lower horizons, which obstruct the penetration of water and sometimes of plant roots also, are quite common. When these impervious layers, often known as *hard-pan,* are covered by shallow top-soil, they present problems for the farmer. In wet weather or under heavy irrigation they become easily waterlogged, and in hot dry weather without water they lose their moisture quickly and become parched.

Types of Agricultural Soil

Agricultural soils are described by their origin, their colour and the texture, *Colluvial* soils are formed from material washed down by rainwater but not transported by streams and rivers. Soils formed from material carried and deposited by streams and rivers are known as *alluvial* soils. *Vertisols* are soils which are formed over their parent rocks without lateral particle movement. The colours of soils vary from almost black (Black Cotton), through shades of red (Red Mediterranean) and brown (Brown Forest) to light yellow.

The texture of soils depends upon the relative proportions of different-sized particles in their make-up. The proportions of different particle sizes can be determined by mechanical analysis, and these mineral components can be classified according to particle size as follows:-

Name	Size Limits (Particle diameters)
Gravel	Above 2 mm
Coarse sand	2.0-0.2 mm
Fine sand	0.2-0.02 mm
Silt	0.02-0.002 mm
Clay	Less than 0.002 mm

The textural descriptions follow the dominant particle sizes in their make-up, so that soils are described as sand, loam, silt or clay, or combinations of these (sandy loam, silty clay/loam etc). The term loam indicates a well-graded component in which no one particle size dominates. The differences between these types are not rigid but the following may be used as a general guide:-

Sandy soils — 60% or more of sands

Loams — Some sand and not more than 30% clay

Clay soils — Over 30% clay and less than 50% sand.

The terms 'light' and 'heavy' refer to the amount of power required to draw a cultivating implement through the soil. In this context, sandy soils tend to be light, loams medium and clays heavy, although clay soils have a lower bulk density (weight of a unit volume, excluding contained water) than sandy soils.

The Chemistry of Soil

The particles of weathered rock which make up the mineral component of soil consist of about fifteen principal elements usually combined with oxygen as oxides and often combined with each other. These major mineral constituents are listed in Table 19.

Table 19 — Approximate quantities of mineral matter in soil		
Element	Symbol	Percentage by weight
Silicon	Si	71.3
Aluminium	Al	13.7
Iron	Fe	6.9
Potassium	K	3.0
Sodium	Na	1.1
Titanium	Ti	1.1
Calcium	Ca	1.0
Magnesium	Mg	0.7
Barium, Phosphorus, Manganese, Sulphur, Chlorine, Fluorine, Chromium and others	Ba, P, Mn, S, Cl, Fl, Cr	0.9
		100.0

The principal elements in the organic component of soil are carbon (C), hydrogen (H) and oxygen (O) combined as carbohydrates, and nitrogen (N) as protein. The quantities of these organic materials vary extensively with the type of soil. Oxygen, carbon and hydrogen are obtained from air and water. Nitrogen is absorbed from the air by plants and released in the soil by the biological decomposition of plant residues.

In addition to oxygen, carbon, hydrogen and nitrogen, plants need potassium, phosphorus, calcium, magnesium, sulphur and iron. The amounts of these nutrients which are used are very small, and most soils contain adequate supplies for plant growth for many years. These nutrients become active ingredients on which plants can feed when they are dissolved in water to form the *soil solution* or when they are retained by adsorption on the surfaces of particles of colloidal clay or of humus. Under natural conditions these active ingredients take part in an almost completely closed biological cycle, passing from the soil into plants through their roots, down to the ground when the plants drop their leaves or die, and then back to the soil through organic decomposition. Agriculture breaks this cycle by removing crops, so that nutrients are lost from the soil, and compensating measures have to be taken to replace the losses, by applying manures and chemical fertilizers. The three most important nutrients which may need to be replenished in soils are potassium, phosphorus and nitrogen, but deficiencies in other nutrients, sometimes used in minute quantities, may also need to be made good.

Nutrient Deficiencies

In irrigated areas, particularly in arid or semi-arid regions, soils may be deficient in organic matter leading to a shortage of nitrogen, and in phosphorus and potassium. These deficiencies injure plant growth, cause poor colour and affect the quality of crop products. Shortages of iron, magnesium and manganese may cause leaves to turn yellow. It is not always easy to diagnose nutrient deficiency correctly, and if in doubt a farmer should seek professional advice.

Salinity

Soils having a high concentration of soluble soils are known as *saline.* They occur most commonly in low-lying areas in arid and semi-arid regions where groundwater, often quite heavily charged with salts in solution, lies near the surface and is subject to intense evaporation leaving the salts in the surface layers of the soil. Salinity can also be produced by irrigating with water containing dissolved salts and maintaining a high water table so that the salts are deposited in the surface soil layers.

Salinity reduces the productivity of crops in various ways, by affecting the soil structure, and making it difficult for plants to absorb water and nutrients. Some plants are more salt tolerant than others. Salt concentrations in the surface layers can be reduced by *leaching,* or washing the salts down to levels below the plant root zone.

The most common soluble salts are those of sodium, potassium, magnesium and calcium. Excesses of the chlorides and sulphates of these elements form a white crust at the soil surface, often known as *white alkali.*

Sodium carbonate, sometimes associated with potassium carbonate, produces *black alkali* soils forming sodium hydroxide which dissolves organic matter causing a dark-coloured crust at the soil surface. These salts are harmful to plant roots, damage the structure of the soil, and may reduce the availability of plant nutrients.

A number of secondary elements needed for plant growth such as manganese, lead, zinc, copper, chromium, iron, fluorine, and others can be harmful if present in excess. Some of these, for example, lead, boron, copper or fluorine, while not necessarily harmful to plants may be toxic in food consumed by human beings or animals.

Acidity and Alkalinity

The acidity and alkalinity of substances are measured by a quantity known as the pH value which refers to the concentration of hydrogen ions (electrically charged particles) in solution. The pH value of water, which is neutral, is 7. Values above 7 are alkaline and below are acid. Alkaline soils are those with pH values greater than 8.5. Acid soils, which are produced from large quantities of organic matter and occur in marshes and swamps, have pH values of 5 or less.

Further Reading

Ivan E. Houk, *Irrigation Engineering,* Vol.I, John Wiley and Son, New York, USA, 1951, Chs.2 and 3.

Orson W. Israelsen, *Irrigation Principles and Practices,* John Wiley and Son, New York, USA, 1958, Ch.11.

Chapter 11
Soil and Water

Soil Moisture

The structure of a soil consists of a framework of solid material enclosing a complex system of pores and channels which provide space within the soil for air and water. When all these spaces are filled with water, the soil is *saturated.* A soil can only remain in a saturated condition if it is below water-table level and cannot drain freely. It may be temporarily saturated above a water-table during and immediately after irrigation or heavy rainfall. The maximum amount of water or moisture which a soil can hold at saturation depends upon the volume of its pore spaces and is known as its *saturation capacity.*

Although regarded as old-fashioned terminology by soil scientists, the moisture in soil can be divided into three classes: *gravity, capillary* and *hygroscopic.* Gravity water can only remain in soil which is above a water-table for a short time, because it drains out under gravity. Capillary water occurs as thin films on the soil particles or as droplets or thin threads within the pore structure. Capillary water is the principal source of water for plant growth, and the amount of water retained by soil after gravity water has drained out is known as the *field capacity.* Hygroscopic water consists of a thin film held on the soil particles so firmly that it is not available for plant growth.

When plants growing in soil are short of water they start to wilt or droop. If water is supplied at this stage, the *wilting point,* they will recover. If, however, they continue without water they will reach a point beyond which they do not recover with additional water. This is known as the *permanent wilting point*; this term is also used to define the level of moisture content in the soil when this state is reached. This level includes all the hygroscopic water and some capillary water. The difference between the moisture content of a soil, and its moisture content at the permanent wilting point is known as the *available water.*

These various soil-moisture quantities are shown diagram-

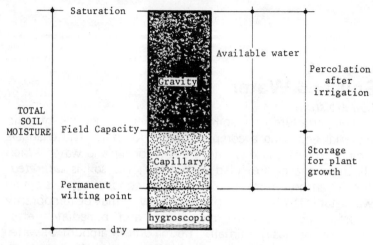

Fig.24 Soil moisture quantities

matically in Figure 24. These quantities are often described as constants, but this is misleading, because they are only constant for a given soil, and vary with the texture and composition of the soil. When soil is irrigated its water content will be raised initially to the saturation level, but if the soil is free draining the "gravity" component of the water will drain away. Gravity water will drain from the root zone in less than a day in coarse sandy soil, or in three or four days in heavy clay soil. This component therefore is not normally counted as being available to crops unless drainage is prevented by underlying hard-pan or by a high water-table.

Table 20 gives typical figures for soil moisture quantities for different types of soil, expressed as percentages by weight of dry soil.

Table 20 — Typical soil moisture quantities Percentages by weight of dry soil			
Soil type	Saturation	Field Capacity	Permanent Wilting Point	Available Water
Fine sand	15-20%	3-6%	1-3%	2-3%
Sandy loam	20-40%	6-14%	3-8%	3-6%
Silt loam	30-50%	12-18%	6-10%	6-8%
Clay loam	40-60%	15-30%	7-16%	8-14%
Clay	40-70%	25-45%	12-20%	13-20%

Available Water

The available water is the water which is accessible to vegetation. As rainfall and irrigation quantities are usually expressed in terms of depth of water it is convenient to express available water in similar terms. To convert the percentages of Table 20 into depths of water it is necessary to know the dry density of the soil. If we call x the dry density of a particular soil in g/cm^3, and f is the percentage by weight of available water, then a cubic metre of the soil will contain 10 fx kg of water. The volume of this quantity of water will be 10 fx litres. This volume in a metre cube of soil is equivalent to a depth of 10 fx mm. Table 21 gives the results of this conversion of available moisture at field capacity for typical soils.

Table 21 — Available water for typical soils at field capacity			
Soil type	Dry Density g/cm^3	Available Water %	mm/metre
Fine sand	1.60-1.76	2-3	30-50
Sandy loam	1.28-1.68	3-6	40-100
Silt loam	1.10-1.50	6-8	60-120
Clay loam	1.10-1.50	8-14	90-210
Clay	1.44-1.54	13-20	190-300

The total available water in a particular soil will be the available water per metre depth multiplied by the depth of the soil. Thus a soil 1.5 m deep with 80 mm available water per metre depth will contain 80 x 1.5 = 120 mm total available water. The same soil 0.5 m deep would contain only 40 mm of available water.

Plant Root Zones

Different plants have different rooting depths, and young plants have much shallower root systems than mature plants. Table 22 gives typical rooting depths for various crops in fertile soil under unrestricted conditions. The figures in the table should be taken only as guides because root patterns depend much on local soil conditions and water availability. Shallow soils must contain shallow root systems. Excessive irrigation, maintaining a high water-table will also tend to produce shallow roots, whereas drought conditions with water available only at considerable depth will encourage deep roots.

Table 22 — Typical root-zone depths					
Depths in metres at full growth					
Shallow		Medium		Deep	
Beans	0.5-0-7	Barley	1.0-1.5	Alfalfa	1.0-2.0
Broccoli	0.4-0.6	Carrots	0.5-1.0	Cotton	1.0-1.7
Cabbage	0.4-0.5	Clover	0.6-0.9	Deciduous	
Cauliflower	0.3-0.6			orchards	1.0-2.0
Grass		Eggplant	0.9-1.2	Maize	1.0-2.0
pasture	0.4-0.6	Grains		Sorghum	1.0-2.0
Lettuce	0.3-0.5	(small)	0.9-1.5	Sugar	
Onions	0.3-0.5	Peas	0.6-1.0	cane	1.0-2.0
Potatoes	0.4-0.6	Peppers	0.5-1.0		
Rice	0.5-0.7	Sweet			
Spinach	0.3-0.5	potatoes	1.0-1.5		
		Tomatoes	0.7-1.5		
		Water			
		melons	1.0-1.5		

Source of data: FAO Irrigation and Drainage Paper No.24, *Crop Water Requirements,* Table 39.

Generally most of the water used by plants is taken from the upper half of the root zone, and because of this only about half of the available water is actually used. This is illustrated in Table 23.

Table 23 — Moisture extraction pattern in plant root zones	
Root zone depth	Percentage of available water used
First quarter	80%
Second quarter	60%
Third quarter	40%
Fourth quarter	20%
	Av. 50%

Irrigation Application

As plants cannot readily use more than half the available moisture in the soil, irrigation is needed when this half is used up. The amount of water to be applied to a particular crop in one irrigation application is therefore half the available moisture in the root zone of the crop when the soil is at field capacity. The interval between applications is determined by the rate at which the plants use the available moisture, as described in Chapter 9. If rain also adds water to the soil, it must be allowed for when estimating irrigation requirements.

The calculation of irrigation requirements will be illustrated by an example. In a particular month of 30 days it has been estimated that a crop will need 240 mm of water, or an average of 8 mm per day. If the soil is clay loam with 120 mm/m available water at field capacity and the effective root depth is 1.35 m, the total available water in the root zone will be 1.35 x 120 = 162 mm. Half this quantity, say 80 mm will be used by the plants, and at a rate of 8 mm per day, the irrigation interval should be 80/8 = 10 days.

If 40 mm of rain falls during one of the 10-day periods, the deficit to be made up at the end of this period will be only 40 mm (80 mm less 40 mm). An irrigation application of 40 mm can be applied now, or, alternatively irrigation could be postponed for 5 days on account of the rainfall, and a full application of 80 mm applied after 15 days interval.

A day by day calculation for readily available soil moisture and irrigation requirements for a month with rainfall on the lines of the above example is given in Figure 25. It has been assumed that the first irrigation in the month is due on the second day and that at the end of the first day the residual readily available water in the soil is 25 mm, requiring an additional 55 mm to bring it to field capacity of 80 mm. It has also been assumed that any water in excess of field

Table 24 — Soil infiltration rates (mm/h)	
Soil	*Infiltration rate*
Clay	1-5
Clay-loam	5-10
Silt-loam	10-20
Sandy loam	20-30
Sand	30-100

capacity drains away too quickly to be used by the crops. These calculations give net irrigation requirements, and gross

DAY	1	2	3	4	5	6	7	8	9	10	11	1
Effective Rain Re mm	-	-	-	-	-	-	-	-	-	-	-	-
Net Gain to Soil Re-Et	-8	-8	-8	-8	-8	-8	-8	-8	-8	-8	-8	-
Irrigation		55										8
Readily available soil moisture-(at end of each day) 100	25	72	64	56	48	40	32	24	16	8	0	7.
80												
60												
40												
20												

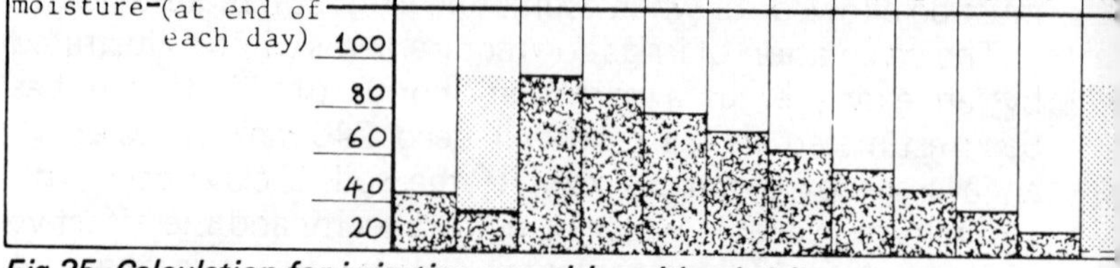

Fig.25 Calculation for irrigation quantities with rainfall

field requirements can be calculated after allowing for losses (as described on page 74). If the field application efficiency is 0.6, the field irrigation application would be 133 mm.

Infiltration Rate

Water enters soil under the action of gravity, and this process is known as *infiltration.* The rate of entry is greatest when the soil is dry at the start of watering, decreasing as the top-soil becomes saturated to a nearly constant rate, which is known as the *infiltration rate* for irrigation. The infiltration rate is expressed in millimetres depth of water per hour, and Table 24 gives typical infiltration rates for different soils.

If the application rate is higher than the infiltration rate, water will be wasted; if it is lower, evaporation losses may be unnecessarily high. The infiltration rate will give the time required to water a piece of land. A soil with an infiltration rate of 20 mm/h will absorb an application of 80 mm in 80/20 = 4 hours. The methods for calculating rates of flow into furrows and corrugations are described in Chapter 5. Soil intake rates for sprinkler irrigation, shown in Table 11, Chapter 7, are slightly lower than infiltration rates, to avoid ponding water at the soil surface.

Irrigation Supply

In the foregoing sections it has been assumed that the farmer has available figures for the characteristics of his soil which he can use for calculating his irrigation requirements. In practice, especially for small scale developments, these figures are unlikely to be available, and much will

3	14	15	16	17	18	19	20	21	22	23	24	25	26	27	28	29	30
0	8	20	-	61	25	13	-	-	-	48	25	-	10	-	-	-	-
0	+12	-8	+53	+17	+5	-8	-8	-8	+40	+17	-8	+2	-8	-8	-8	-8	
									16								
0	80	80	72	80	80	80	72	64	72	80	80	72	74	66	58	50	42

depend on the farmer's judgement and trial and error in the field in determining his irrigation quantities. But some knowledge of the methods of calculating these quantities is extremely useful, because by making appropriate assumptions from the tables in this chapter quantities can be calculated which will serve as a check against conclusions reached in the field by trial and error.

While it is convenient to think of irrigation applications in terms of depths of water it is difficult to measure these depths without scientific equipment, and the farmer in the field needs to relate his irrigation requirements to quantities which he can measure and with which he is familiar. The most easily measurable quantity is time, if it is not required to great accuracy, and many irrigation systems are operated on the basis of time. A farmer may know from experience that it takes him half a day to irrigate a particular field. He may qualify this by adding that it holds only when his source of supply is running properly; in other words, when his supply channel is flowing full. If his supply is reduced the same field may take a whole day to irrigate. In the example of Figure 25 an irrigation application rate of 6.5 mm/h has been assumed so that a full application of 80 mm takes 12 hours. With a constant source of supply, smaller applications take proportionately less time. If the field application efficiency is 0.6 the gross rate of application will be 6.5/0.6 = 10.8 mm/h. If the area of the irrigated field is 2 hectares, the field water supply needed will be:-

$$\frac{2 \times 10,000 \times 10.8}{3,600} = 60 \text{ litres per second}$$

In this way a farmer can check that his source of water is sufficient to water the area of the field.

Further Reading

Ivan E. Houk, *Irrigation Engineering,* Vol.I, John Wiley and Sons, New York, USA, 1951, Ch.4.
G.V. Jacks, *Soil,* Thomas Nelson and Sons Ltd, London, England 1963, Ch.IV.

Chapter 12
Drainage

The term drainage is used here to describe all processes whereby surplus water is removed from agricultural land. It includes both the internal drainage of soils, and the collection and disposal of surface run-off.

Soil Drainage

As has been described in Chapter 11, it is the capacity of soils for holding water which enables plants to grow by drawing water and nutrients in solution in the water from the soils through their root systems. Since air is also necessary to these processes, soils should not be permanently saturated with water. A good soil therefore has good internal drainage characteristics, which means that water must be able to move fairly easily through the soil so that excess water can be removed when required.

Heavy clay soils are poor draining; light sandy soils are free draining. If soils drain too freely, they will be wasteful of irrigation water, and this can be a problem if water supplies are limited. The best soils are those of medium texture, composed of a mixture of large and small particle sizes, and deep enough (say over 40 cms) to have sufficient water holding capacity to sustain plant life for a week or ten days.

A type of soil which occurs extensively in tropical and sub-tropical regions consists of a shallow, reasonably permeable upper layer, which may be only 10 cm deep, lying over a very dense impermeable clay (often known as hard pan). This soil has serious drainage problems. Because the upper layer, which may have good internal drainage characteristics, is shallow, it is quickly saturated by rainfall or irrigation. As surplus water cannot drain easily through the underlying impermeable clay, the top soil may remain waterlogged for many days or weeks.

Wherever possible land chosen for agricultural development should have naturally well-drained soils. Freedom of choice is not always possible, and a farmer may often have to use poorly-drained soils. With some poorly-drained soils measures can be taken to improve their drainage. Cultivation processes such as ploughing and hoeing will improve the soil at the surface, and heavy sub-soil can be broken up and mixed with lighter top-soil by digging or ripping. Soils which drain freely but too slowly, such as some heavy alluvial soils, can be improved by sub-soil drains, which may be stone and gravel, brushwood, specially made tile drain pipes, or slotted plastic pipe, laid 80 cm or more below the surface. To be effective, sub-soil drains are laid at 20 or 30 m intervals and this can be expensive. Low-lying land with a naturally high water table may need deep boundary drains to collect and remove sub-soil drainage water.

Surface Drainage

In addition to the removal of surplus water from within the soil, consideration should be given to the disposal of surface run-off arising from rainfall or, sometimes, from excessive irrigation. Where natural rainfall is light, say less than 500 mm in a season, most of the rain is absorbed on the land, but heavy storm water will occasionally need to be removed. If the land is furrowed or corrugated, water will collect in the furrows and move down them, so that a drainage ditch is needed to collect this water. If the land is irrigated by basin flooding, outlets are needed for draining the basins. Where cultivated land is adjacent to higher slopes which produce their own run-off after rainfall, it will be necessary to provide a protective catch drain along the boundary of the cultivation to prevent the run-off from the higher land sweeping over the cultivation.

Farm Drainage

Field drainage will be effective only if the drainage water is removed to a point where it is no longer a nuisance on the farm or to neighbouring properties. It is important, therefore, that a drainage system should be designed to deliver into natural drainage outlets, or into communally accepted disposal areas. Figure 26 shows a drainage layout for a 25 hectare farm unit and Figure 27, methods for providing field drainage.

Design of Drainage Systems

Surface drainage systems are designed to evacuate surplus water at a rate which is calculated or estimated from data

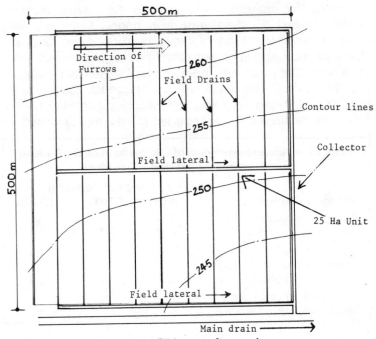

Fig.26 Drainage layout for a 25-hectare farm unit

about local conditions. It is usually based on the maximum surface run-off which may be expected after heavy rainfall, and for a small catchment area, this can be calculated from the formula:

Q = C i A
where
Q is in litres per second
C is a coefficient of run-off
i = rainfall intensity in mm/h
A = area of catchment in ha.

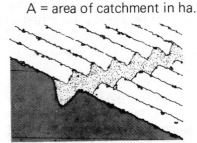
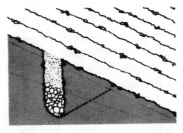
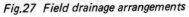

Fig.27 Field drainage arrangements

The rainfall intensity of a storm is the total amount of rainfall divided by the duration in hours. The coefficient C varies with the topography, vegetation cover, and soil characteristics, and it is not easy to select the correct value for a particular situation. Table 25 may be used as a guide for the choice of C, for small catchments under 250 hectares, but because it can vary so much with local conditions, the figures in the table must be regarded as very approximate.

Table 25 — Approximate values of C in the formula Q = C i A for small catchments less than 250 hectares

Nature of Catchment	Slope of catchment		
	0-5%	5-10%	10-30%
Poor soil cover, little or no vegetation, low infiltration	1.8	1.9	2.2
Land with fair to good soils, 50% vegetation or cultivation, medium infiltration	1.2	1.4	1.7
Deep soils, forest or dense vegetation, high infiltration	0.8	1.0	1.2

Figures for storm rainfall intensities are not always easy to obtain. In the tropics and sub-tropics average storm rainfall intensities between 20 and 50 mm/h are quite common. For short periods of half an hour or less, intensities are much greater and may be 200 mm/h or more. With a rainfall intensity of 30 mm/h on a 10 ha catchment with C = 1.4, the estimated run-off from Q = C i A would be 420 l/s.

In some situations, where flat agricultural land can accept temporary flooding, it may only be necessary to remove surplus water gradually, say over a period of 48 hours. If, for example, a typical heavy storm on a 10 ha catchment amounted to a total of 150 mm in 5 hours (i.e. average intensity 30 mm/h), and the soil were already saturated at the start of the storm, the volume of water to be removed would be 15,000 m³. To remove this in 48 hours would require an evacuation rate of 86.6 l/sec.

Drainage channels are usually trapezoidal in cross section, with side slopes varying between 3:1 (horizontal: vertical) for sandy soils and 1½:1 for stiff clays. The full supply level in field drains should be kept below the root zone of crops, which may mean that the water level is 1 or 2 metres below

Table 26 – Drain Channel capacities in litres/second for various channel slopes and sections.

Channels are trapezoidal with side slopes 1½:1 (horizontal:vertical) and roughness coefficient 0.035

	Bed width (B) and water depth (D) in metres							
B	0.10	0.15	0.20	0.25	0.30	0.40	0.50	0.60
D	0.15	0.25	0.30	0.40	0.50	0.65	0.85	1.00
Channel slope								
1/10,000 0.01%	2.5	9.3	16	33	59	121	243	378
1/5,000 0.02%	3.6	13	23	47	84	172	345	518
1/2,000 0.05%	5.6	21	36	74	133	271	545	845
1/1,000 0.1%	7.8	30	51	107	190	390	770	1200
1/500 0.2%	11	42	71	148	266	540	1090	1690
1/333 0.3%	13.5	51	87	183	330	670	1330	2065
1/250 0.4%	15.5	59	100	212	380	765	1540	2385*
1/200 0.5%	17	66	113	237	422	855	1720*	2670*
1/100 1.0%	24	94	160	330	595*	1210*	2430*	3775*

*Velocities greater than 1 m/s

adjacent ground level, and the excavated drain section will be very much larger than the required water cross-section.

Drainage channels are designed according to hydraulic theory in the same way as irrigation supply channels (see Chapter 14), which means that for a given land slope, flow, and soil material, there may be several possible solutions. Table 26 gives flows in litres/sec for a range of channel slopes and sections with side slopes 1½:1 and with an assumed roughness coefficient of 0.035.

A high roughness coefficient at 0.035 (see Table 28) has been used in the table because drains tend to be obstructed with weed and rubbish. To avoid risk of erosion, the velocity of flow should always be calculated by dividing the discharge by the water cross-sectional area. Safe velocities for different earth materials range from 0.5 m/s for fine sands, to 1.1 m/s for stiff clays and 1.5 m/s for cobbles and shingle. In general it is advisable to ensure that velocities are less than 1 m/s.

Drainage and Salinity

The importance of water table control in helping to overcome the dangers of salinity in some arid parts of the world has already been mentioned in Chapter 6. Where irrigation is practised in these areas, effective land drainage is essential to keep the water moving downwards through the soil, to prevent the accumulation of harmful salts at the soil surface. There are many examples in India, Pakistan and the Middle East of large areas of previously fertile irrigated land now covered with a white crust of salts, abandoned and incapable of supporting crops.

Soil Erosion

Soil erosion occurs through too rapid surface drainage of erodible soils, resulting from the removal of protective vegetation. Surface run-off after heavy rainfall picks up and carries away soil particles, and in this way valuable fertile land is destroyed.

The problem is more widespread in tropical countries, where intense or high rainfall is experienced and where cultivation and alluvial panning activities may be carried out without advice or against the law in remote areas. For example, the clearing of primary jungle in mountainous parts of Malaya and the cultivation of vegetables, maize, rice, rubber trees, and other crops without soil protection has resulted in erosion taking the top soil and carrying it to the flat land in the valleys. This has the double disadvantage of denuding the higher land of valuable top soil and also of depositing it in a haphazard fashion on the lower land, and creating serious problems of silting and consequent flooding in the river systems.

Further Reading

Bruce Withers and Stanley Vipond, *Irrigation: Design and Practice,* B.T. Batsford Ltd, 4 Fitzhardinge Street, London W1H 0AH, England, 1974, pp.156-188.

Chapter 13
Source Development

Water for irrigation can be obtained from a variety of sources. It can be diverted from springs, streams or rivers, lifted from rivers and lakes, or drawn from wells and boreholes. All fresh water, whether it is on the surface of the land or underground, originated from rainfall. Surface run-off from rainfall collects in rivulets and streams, eventually combining into a single main stream or river. An area served in this way by a single drainage outflow is known as a drainage basin or catchment area.

A dam built across a river will collect run-off from the river's catchment area above the dam, and this provides a reservoir which can be used for irrigation. This principle of collecting water is used in many large irrigation schemes. There is a finite limit to the number of river systems in the world which can be treated in this way, and there are very large areas of semi-arid land supporting subsistence cultivation where there are no convenient river systems which could be developed.

This is not to say that there are no drainage systems in these semi-arid areas. There are, but because of a number of reasons associated with the physical characteristics of the area, only a very small part of the precipitation on the land surface ever appears as outflow. The general drainage slope of the terrain may be too flat so that water moves over it slowly and is all evaporated on the way. The land surface may consist of shallow porous soils overlying impermeable material which take up most of the rainfall and return it to the air by evaporation. The basin may consist of predominantly porous rock formations which absorb the rainfall to feed underground reservoirs outside the basin. Under any or all of these conditions, the total surface run-off in a year will consist only of surplus run-off following exceptionally heavy rainfall, and this yield may be too low to justify the construction of a dam and reservoir. Run-off from small catchments in semi-arid areas, intercepted and collected before it is lost, can provide a valuable source of water. Run-off farming, described in Chapter 4, is one example of this; small catchment storage is another.

Small Catchment Storage

There are many parts of the world where subsistence cultivation is carried out with an average annual rainfall of 500 mm, which means that the actual rainfall in dry years will be around 300 mm. Because of the low and unreliable rainfall and poor soils, about 10 hectares of land are needed to produce the staple crop (millet or sorghum usually) that a rural farmer needs to support himself and his family. This low rainfall is insufficient to grow tomatoes, egg-plant, peppers and other vegetables to supplement the staple food and add interest and nutrition to the diet.

What could a farmer with 10 hectares of land and without much scientific knowledge do under these conditions to improve this situation? He could set aside say 1000 square metres of his land (one per cent of the total) for catchment irrigation. Of this 1000 square metres, 700 square metres would be prepared as a catchment apron, from which run-off would be fed into a catchment tank, and 300 square metres would be used as a vegetable garden, irrigated by watering can from the tank.

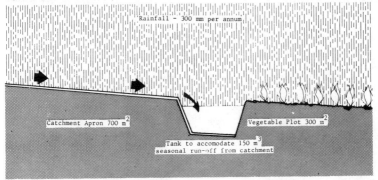

Fig.28 Micro-irrigation system

In a dry year, with 300 mm of rain, the catchment apron would receive 210 cubic metres of water. Some of this water would be absorbed by the soil of the apron itself, some would return to the air by direct evaporation and some, say 150 cubic metres, could be collected. If, allowing for losses, 100 cubic metres of water from the tank could be used on the vegetable garden, the garden would then receive 300 mm of direct rainfall plus 330 mm from the tank, making a total of 630 mm. Figure 28 illustrates this principle.

The effectiveness of this *micro-irrigation* system will depend upon the capacity of the catchment apron for delivering run-off and on the efficiency of the tank for storage. A very suitable natural surface for a catchment apron is bare rock, and there are situations where this can be used. If an earth surface is to be used, it should consist of well-compacted heavy soil, and the slope chosen so that water will run off more quickly than it is absorbed, but not so steep that erosion develops. In any case, the run-off should be arrested by a silt trap before it is admitted to the storage tank. Artificial waterproofing of a catchment apron can be done, using concrete, brickwork, masonry, bitumen or polythene.

The storage tank should be water-tight. If excavated in heavy alluvial soil, it may be sufficiently water-tight without lining. But in most soils, lining will be necessary. This can be done with brickwork, concrete masonry and cement plaster, or with membrane materials such as synthetic rubber, PVC and polythene. Concrete or masonry lining may be expensive, and call for skills which may not be readily available to the farmer. Of the synthetic materials polythene is the least expensive. Figure 29 shows one type of catchment tank construction, with a pillar-supported roof.

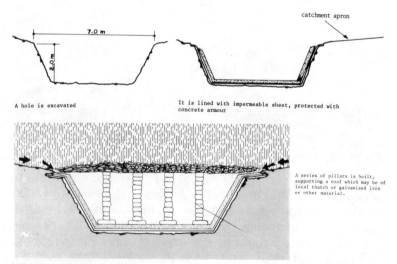

catchment apron

7.0 m

2.0 m

A hole is excavated

It is lined with impermeable sheet, protected with concrete armour

A series of pillars is built, supporting a roof which may be of local thatch or galvanised iron or other material.

Fig.29 Catchment tank construction

Streams and Rivers

In upland areas where streams flow for at least six months in the year, water can be diverted for irrigation. In some cases a direct diversion can be made by excavating a channel leading from the stream just above a natural barrier. More usually it will be necessary to build a diversion structure across the stream to pond up the water so that it can be fed into an irrigation channel.

A diversion structure may be either (a) a *weir,* intended, and therefore strong enough to be overtopped when the stream is in flood, or (b) a *groin* constructed across only a part of the stream's bed, or (c) a *low dam* with a *wash-out section* designed to be destroyed when the stream is in flood. Examples of these diversions are shown in Figures 30 to 32. Weirs and small dams can be constructed with boulders, brushwood, or earth, or combinations of these. They can also be constructed with sawn timber, masonry, brickwork or concrete.

It is very easy to under-estimate the strength needed to resist water pressure and the energy of flowing water. Many small diversion structures are constructed temporarily in the knowledge that they will be destroyed by flood flows. Sometimes part of the structure may be permanent and part temporary, as with the dam and wash-out section. A simple form of construction which can be permanent is with the use of *gabions,* which are baskets made of heavy duty chicken wire or wire mesh, placed in position in the stream bed and then filled with boulders (Figure 33). A full gabion 2 x 1 x 1 metres weighs about 1½ tons.

In planning to use water from a stream for irrigation we must know how much water is needed, and if the stream is capable of providing this water for the whole of the irrigation season. We have discussed a method for calculating the water required for irrigation in Chapter 11. Streams in tropical and sub-tropical regions have a tendency to flow violently and liberally during the rains, and for the flow to drop rapidly and progressively as soon as the rains are over. Their flow patterns may also vary considerably from one year to the next, and it is therefore important to have records of the flow of the stream for as long a period as possible. Streams fed from springs usually have less variable flows than streams which are not.

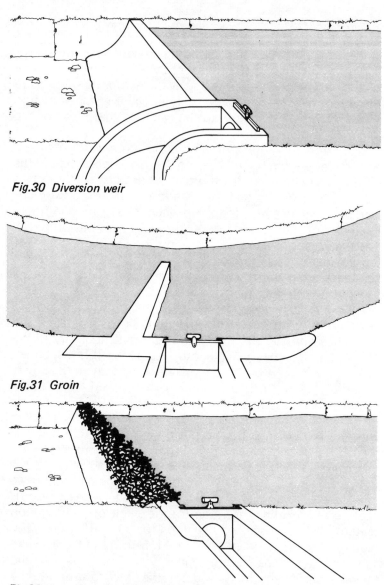

Fig.30 Diversion weir

Fig.31 Groin

Fig.32 Low dam with washout section .

Most countries have a Water Development or Water Resources Department or Organisation which carries out systematic measurements of the principal rivers and streams, and collects and collates all hydrological data for the country.

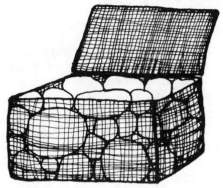

Fig.33 Gabion filled with stone, lid open

This department or organisation should be consulted for any information about a stream intended for irrigation. If no information is available about this particular stream, a hydrologist may be able to make estimates of yield by comparison with an adjacent stream for which there are records. In any case, as soon as a farmer contemplates using a stream for which there are no records, he should take steps to start records.

Gauging a stream at a point where a diversion is proposed involves two activities. One, which is easy and requires no special technical skill is the regular measurement of water levels by reading the height of the water (usually daily) on a *staff gauge,* which is a post or plate placed vertically in the stream and graduated in metres and centimetres.

The second activity is the actual measurement of the flow, which requires technical knowledge and equipment, if it is to be determined accurately. This is done by one of the methods described in Appendix D, and is best carried out by the officials and organisation equipped for this sort of work. If this is not possible, then an approximate method should be used, but again, not without technical advice and assistance.

The most important information needed about the stream flow is its steady discharge or rate of flow. If the irrigation requirement at the point of diversion (which will include conveyance losses as described at the end of this chapter) is 15 litres per second and the water is needed at this rate every day for 5 months, the stream must be capable of producing this for all of this period. This can only be determined from daily records for as long a period as possible. The use of a rating curve or a measuring weir is explained in Appendix D.

The construction of weirs, dams or barrages on large streams and rivers is usually undertaken by public agencies or large private enterprises, and is not work which can be done by the single farmer or small village unit without assistance. Under certain conditions it is possible to divert water into irrigation off-takes without a structure across the river. This can be done where the river channel is on a very flat slope in an alluvial plain, with water-level almost at ground level at the river bank, and if the land is sloping away from the river. Under these conditions a cut in the river bank will allow water to flow on to the adjacent land. An interesting example of this method assisted by the effect of ocean tides is to be found in the swamp estuaries of the Great and Little Scarcies Rivers in Sierra Leone, West Africa. Fresh water in these rivers, elevated by the rising tide, is allowed to flow through cuts in the river banks into rice fields.

A far more usual situation is to find good irrigable land several metres above the water level of a river. If there is no diversion structure on the river such as a dam or a weir further upstream to raise the water above the level of the land, then the use of some water-lifting device will be called for. Methods of lifting water are described in Chapter 15.

Wells and Boreholes

The capacity of a well or borehole for supplying irrigation water is usually not very great. There are exceptions and some large irrigation schemes depend on borehole water. For small-scale operations borehole supplies tend to be too costly, but shallow wells are feasible sources, and are used in many countries. Here we use 'well' to mean a wide hole one metre or more in diameter, excavated by hand, and 'borehole' to mean a narrow hole drilled by machine.

The yield of a well or borehole is the maximum rate at which water can be extracted, and this often varies with the time of year. It is important to know the lowest yield during the period when irrigation water will be needed. Some methods for measuring yield are described in Appendix D.

Chapter 14
Channels and Pipelines

Irrigation Channels

The simplest method of conveying water from a source to land to be irrigated is by allowing it to flow under gravity in channels or canals made of earth. While the size and slope of a channel can be determined by trial and error, it is helpful to know something about the theory of flow. For very small channels (less that 1 l/s capacity) the cross-section can be V- or U- shaped; the most usual channel cross-section is trapezoidal. These three channel sections are shown in Figure 34.

Type of Channel	V-Section	Semicircular	Trapezoidal
Section Water depth - = D Side slope = k:1 Water surface width = W	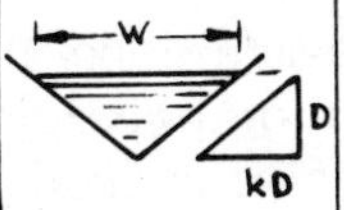 $W = 2kD$	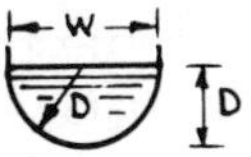 $W = 2D$	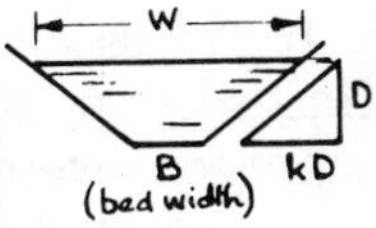 $W = B + 2kD$
Area, A In terms of W,D,B : In terms of k,D,B :	$A = \dfrac{WD}{2}$ $A = kD^2$	$A = \pi D^2$ $= 3.142\,D^2$ —	$A = \dfrac{W+B}{2}\cdot D$ $A = BD + kD^2$
Wetted Perimeter, P	$P = 2D\sqrt{1+k^2}$	$P = \pi D$ $= 3.142\,D$	$P = B + 2D\sqrt{1+k^2}$
Hydraulic Mean Radius, R	$R\,\dfrac{kD}{2\sqrt{1+k^2}}$	$R = D$	$R = \dfrac{BD + kD^2}{B + 2D\sqrt{1+k^2}}$

Fig.34 The hydraulic characteristics of channel sections

In straight-sided channels it is convenient to define the slope of the sides, and this is usually expressed as the horizontal to vertical ratio of the slope. Thus a side slope of 2:1 would be set out by measuring 2 metres horizontally and 1 metre vertically. In an earth channel, the side slopes should be as steep as possible without being unstable in water. Slopes can be steeper in stiff clays than in soft sands. Table 27 gives suitable side slopes for different materials.

Table 27 — Suitable channel side slopes for different earth materials	
	Slope
Material	Horizontal/Vertical
Sand	3:1
Sandy loam	2½:1 to 2:1
Clay loam	2:1 to 1½:1
Clays	2:1 to 1:1
Gravel	1½:1 to 1:1
Rock	1:1 to ¼:1

If k is used to denote the side slope, then the area of the cross-section of a triangular or trapezoidal channel can be expressed in terms of k and the water depth D, as in Figure 34.

The *wetted perimeter (P)* of a water cross-section is the length of the boundary between the water and the sides of the channel, and expressions for P are also given in Figure 34. The *hydraulic mean radius (R)* of a channel is obtained by dividing the sectional area (A) by the wetted perimeter (thus R = A/P).

The rate of flow (Q) in a channel in cubic metres per second, the velocity of flow (V) in metres per second and the water sectional area (A) in square metres, are related in the equation Q = AV. If the flow is required in litres per second, then Q = 1000 AV. Thus for a given section area, the flow Q varies with the velocity V. The velocity of flow depends on (a) the slope of the channel, so that the steeper the slope the greater the velocity, and (b) the friction between the water and the bed and sides of the channel which depends on the material used to form the channel. The friction factor is defined by a coefficient of roughness, *n,* which varies in the range 0.01 to 0.05. Table 28 gives values of *n* for some typical conditions.

Table 28 — Coefficients of roughness (n) for different types of channel	
Type of channel	n
Earth, straight and uniform	0.016-0.025
Earth, winding and sluggish ⎤	
Rough stoney beds, weeds on earth banks ⎦	0.025-0.040
Channels with weeds and bushes	0.025-0.035
Concrete	0.012-0.018

The velocity of flow is related to the coefficient of roughness, the hydraulic mean radius and the slope in Manning's formula:-

$$V = \frac{1}{n} \ R^{2/3} \ S^{1/2}$$

In designing a supply channel we usually know the flow required and wherever possible the slope of the channel should be approximately the slope of the land on the proposed channel alignment. Knowing the material in which the channel will be dug, we can make a suitable choice of roughness coefficient (Table 28). If we decide on a trapezoidal section, we can select an appropriate side slope (Table 27), and we then have to choose dimensions which will give us a velocity V which will satisfy the supply required (Q = AV). If the velocity is too great the material in the bed and sides of the channel will be eroded by the water, and safe maximum velocities for different materials are suggested in Table 29.

Table 29 — Suggested maximum water velocities for different earth materials	
Material	Velocity m/s
Sand	0.5
Sandy Loam	0.6
Alluvial silt	0.8
Loam	0.9
Clay	1.2
Gravel	1.2

It will be clear from the foregoing that the design of a channel can be quite a laborious mathematical process, and wherever possible assistance should be sought from technical advisers or text books and charts. Figure 35 is an example of a design chart, for a range of channel sizes, slopes and

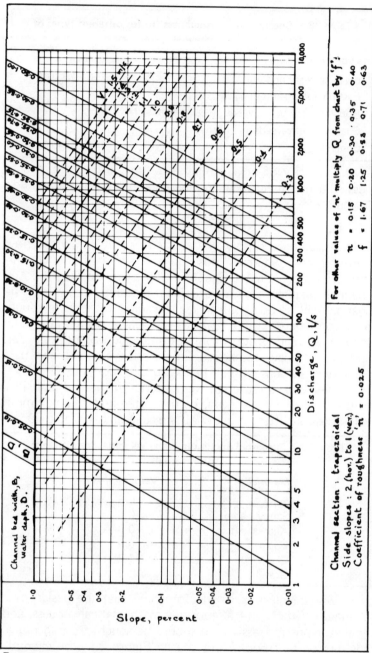

Fig.35 Irrigation canal design chart

water velocities. This chart has been based on an assumed roughness coefficient, *n,* of 0.025 for trapezoidal channels with side slopes 2:1. Suppose, for example, we require a channel in a clay-loam soil to carry 60 l/s on land sloping at 0.1% (1 in 1,000). The vertical 60 l/s line intersects the horizontal 0.1% slope line at a point between two typical channel lines of the following dimensions:-

	(1)	(2)
Bed width, m	0.10	0.15
Water depth, m	0.25	0.30

Either of these sections will be approximately correct, but to be on the safe side we should choose the larger, which will actually carry 80 l/s. It will therefore carry 60 l/s at a reduced water depth.

In selecting a design, we should also check that the velocity of flow is less than the maximum safe velocity to avoid erosion. Velocity lines are shown on Figure 35 for this purpose. Channels which are lined with concrete, bricks or stone can take higher velocities, up to about 2 m/s, and this will allow smaller cross-sections for a given flow. But lining is costly and is not usually feasible except for short distances.

It should be noted that the lines on Figure 35 apply to channels with a roughness coefficient of 0.025. The same channel design lines can be used for other roughness co-efficients, but the flow figures will then be altered proportionately. A channel with bed width 0.15 m and water depth 0.30 m will carry 100 l/s at a slope of 0.15% according to Figure 35, with a roughness coefficient, *n,* of 0.025. If *n* is 0.035, the capacity of the channel would be:

$$100 \times \frac{0.025}{0.035} = 71.4 \text{ l/s}$$

If *n* is 0.015, the capacity of the channel would be:

$$100 \times \frac{0.025}{0.015} = 167 \text{ l/s}$$

Construction of Channels

Before a channel can be designed a survey must be carried

out to determine the alignment or route of the channel and the fall in land level along its length. A field channel normally delivers water through an outlet or control and the water level in the channel should be 15 to 20 cm higher than the highest point in the field which is served by that outlet. This height is known as the *command* height in the field channel. If there are several outlets, each one should be checked for command height.

It will be clear that if a channel is to deliver water on relatively flat land, it must be built up above ground level, and earth must be borrowed from the edge of the field or elsewhere to form the channel. Where the channel is serving as a conveyor with no outlets it is usually designed and constructed so that the water level is approximately at ground level, and the material excavated to form the channel is placed on either side to give the necessary bank height above water level, which should be half the full supply water depth in the channel. This height is known as *free board.*

The water level at the head of a channel will be the water level at its tail plus the drop along its length. If the channel is carrying water from a stream with a weir, the water level at the head must be no higher than the minimum level in the stream at the weir. If the channel is taking water from a pumped supply, the water level at the head of the channel will govern the pump lift needed. It may happen that the designed drop along the channel is too little for the lie of the land, and if this is the case, drop structures or artificial waterfalls will be constructed in the channel, in concrete, masonry or brickwork, so that the earth sections of the channel can still follow the best design slope.

To excavate a trapezoidal channel, the bed width and total width at ground level are set out on the ground with pegs and string. If the earth is firm, the bed section is dug first to the full depth required, placing the earth on both sides, at least 15 cm outside the lines of the edges of the channel. The sides are then excavated and formed to the required side slopes. It is important to place the earth outside the final edges of the channel to prevent it rolling back into the excavation before it has been consolidated. Small channels are best excavated by hand, but hand work can be assisted by ploughing with a ridger type plough to break a hard compacted surface.

Channel Conveyance Losses

Some of the water flowing in an earth channel is lost on its way by evaporation from the water surface, by evapotranspiration through vegetation growing on the channel banks, and by percolation or seepage through the bed and sides of the channel. The evaporation from the surface of a channel is relatively small and usually less than 1% of the channel flow. The evapotranspiration and seepage losses can be quite considerable. They are very difficult to estimate because they depend so much on local conditions. They can be determined by measuring the difference between the flow into and out of a channel, and measurements show channel losses on large irrigation schemes to be of the order of 60% to 70% of the water supplied. On single well-maintained channels in impervious material they may be much less, but in general 50% to 70% losses may be expected in earth channels. In highly permeable materials channels need to be lined. Various materials can be used for lining, such as concrete, stone, masonry, brickwork, asphalt. Channels can also be lined with buried membranes of butyl rubber, PVC and polythene sheeting, and sprayed bitumen. All lining methods tend to be expensive.

Pipelines

While long pipelines are expensive and therefore not usually feasible for irrigation supplies, it may be necessary to carry an open-channel supply through a pipe for short distances, such as across a road or drainage gully. The carrying capacity of a pipe depends upon its sectional area, the roughness of its inside surface and the head or difference of pressure of the water between entering and leaving the pipe. Head is lost in the pipe through friction, which varies with the material from which the pipe is made. Common materials for irrigation pipework are concrete, asbestos-cement, steel and poly-vinyl-chloride (PVC). The charts in Figures 36 to 39 show the relationship between head losses in metres per 100 metre length of pipe, and pipe flows in litres per second for a range of pipe sizes for these four different materials, when the pipes are flowing full.

As an example in the use of these charts, suppose we need to carry a 20 l/s supply in a pipe 40 m long. If we use an asbestos-cement pipe 20 cm dia, the 20 cm line on Figure 37

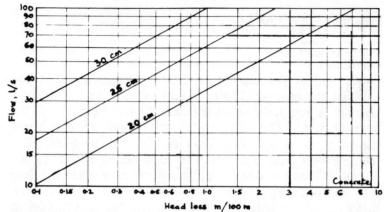

Fig.36 Concrete pipe design chart for various pipe sizes measured by internal diameter

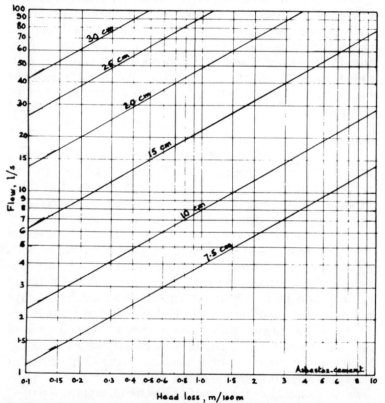

Fig.37 Asbestos-cement pipe design chart for various pipe sizes measured by internal diameter

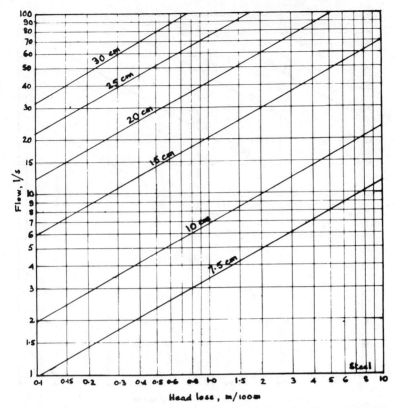

Head loss, m/100m

Fig.38 Steel pipe design chart for various pipe sizes measured by internal diameter

cuts the 20 l/s line at 0.2 m/100 m head loss. The total head lost through the pipe will be 0.2 x 0.40 = 0.08 m. This means that if the pipe is used to bridge a gap in a channel system, the water level in the channel at the downstream end of the pipe will be 8 cm below that at the upstream end. If a 15 cm dia. asbestos-cement pipe were used, the head "drop" would be a lot greater, in fact 0.84 x 0.40 = 0.34 m (Figure 37). If a PVC pipe were used, with less friction, the head lost would be, from Figure 39, 0.068 m for a 20 cm pipe and 0.27 m for a 15 cm pipe. The choice of pipe will depend on local site conditions and the availability and cost of piping. Where the land is very flat and head losses need to be kept to a minimum, a larger diameter pipe should be used.

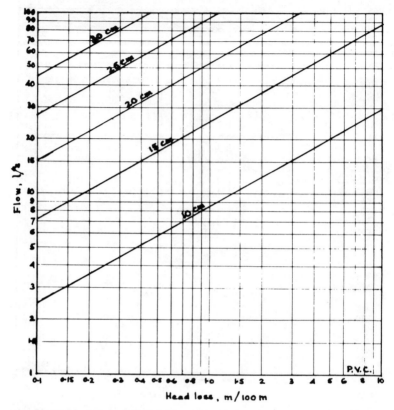

Fig.39 PVC pipe design chart for various pipe size measured by internal diameter

If there is adequate fall along the line of the canal, then a smaller diameter pipe can be used.

Further Reading

There are many standard text books on the theory of open channel and pipe hydraulics, and a technical library should therefore be consulted.

Chapter 15
Water Lifting

While the earliest irrigation schemes in history probably depended only on the gravity flow of water, it was not long before man became aware of the need to lift water for irrigation, and many devices were developed for this purpose in different parts of the world using man or animal power. The advent of mechanical power and modern machinery revolutionised the technology of water lifting, enabling water to be raised to heights and in quantities enormously greater than had hitherto been possible. Cheap oil fuel and hydro-electric power where available contributed to the popularity of power driven pumping, and pump schemes for irrigation were developed wherever they were found to be financially and economically viable.

The success of the mechanical pumping system has, however, been marred by the very high incidence of failure where it has been applied inappropriately to agricultural communities which cannot manage installations which are too dependent on imported equipment and spare parts and on skilled labour which is in very short supply. Because of this, and because of the increasing costs of oil fuels and other sources of power, research and development resources are now being developed on quite a large scale, to re-discovering the use of man, animal and wind power for water lifting, and to improving traditional technology with the aid of modern knowledge and materials.

In this chapter we summarise briefly the different types of water-lifting devices available for irrigation, without entering into great detail. Useful references to these subjects will be found at the end of this chapter.

Manual Water Lifting

The simplest form of manual device is the water container which is filled and carried to the plants to be irrigated. In the Central Valleys of Oaxaca, Mexico, where the water table is 1 to 10 m below ground surface farmers open wells in the fields at intervals of 20 to 40 m. A 10 to 14 litre clay or metal vessel is used to draw water from these wells. It has been estimated that a farmer can water up to 400 square metres in an 8-hour working day in this way. The watering can (Figure 20) is another vessel used in this way. Water can be raised by scooping, and a device for doing this is shown in Figure 40.

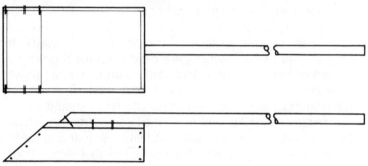

Fig.40 Irrigation by scoop

Man-powered Systems

A system commonly seen throughout the Middle and Far East uses the principle of the lever to raise a bucket from a well or irrigation channel (Figure 41), known by its Arabic name as the 'shadouf'. The Indian 'dall' or 'auge' (Figure 42) uses the lever in a similar way.

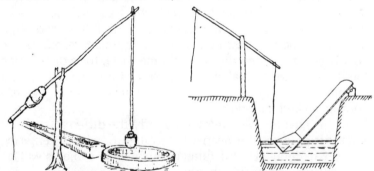

Fig.41 The beam and bucket   *Fig.42 The Indian 'Dall'*

The Archimedian Screw, said to have been invented by Archimedes about 200 B.C. is shown in Figures 43 and 44. It is still used in Egypt and India, for low lifts of between 0.25 m and 1.30 m. Limited to working between fairly constant operating levels, it is one of the more efficient water lifting machines in terms of output for energy input.

Fig.43 Archimedean screw (Photo: Douglas Dickens)

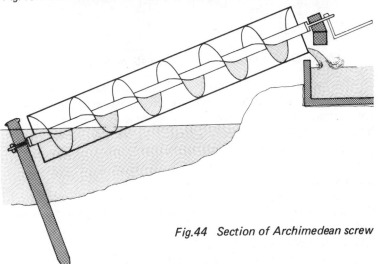

Fig.44 Section of Archimedean screw

Hand operated chain and bucket pumps are shown in Figures 45 and 46. They both consist of continuous chains suspended and rotated vertically. In the former case discs or washers are attached to the chain, which passes through a vertical tube in its upward movement; in the latter case buckets are attached to the chain. The chain pump was used extensively in mines in Europe in the 16th Century. More recently it has been developed in China.

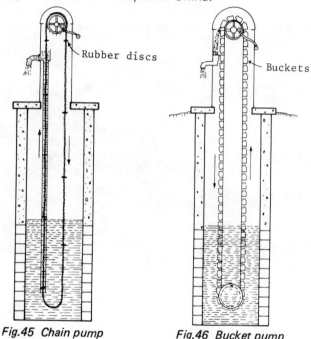

Fig.45 Chain pump   Fig.46 Bucket pump

The reciprocating pump is the type of hand pump most widely used, primarily for community water supply, but also for irrigation. The origins of the reciprocating pump are believed to date from about 275 B.C. A wooden reciprocating pump was used as a ship's pump in the early Greek and Roman navies, and archeological remains of reciprocating pumps from late Roman times have been found in Europe. Wooden reciprocating pumps were in common use in Europe throughout the 16th and 17th centuries and in the 19th and early 20th centuries metal hand pumps were manufactured on a large scale in the United States and Europe.

The main parts of a reciprocating hand pump are shown in Figure 47. The handle, connected to the pump rod, moves the plunger up and down inside the pump cylinder. As the plunger rises, water is drawn through a non-return valve at the bottom of the cylinder, into the cylinder. On the downward stroke, the bottom valve closes and the water passes

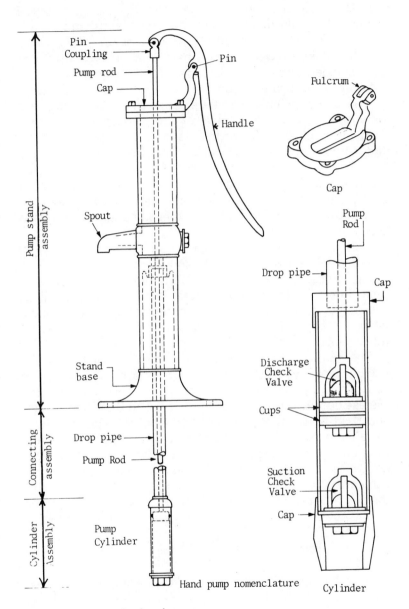

Fig.47 Reciprocating hand pump

through a second non-return valve in the plunger, to the upper side of the plunger. On the next upward stroke, this water is forced up the drop pipe (or rising pipe), while a second intake of water is drawn in through the bottom of the cylinder. Water is thus raised to the pump head and discharged through the spout.

The pump cylinder may be placed below the pump stand or within it, depending on the depth of the water surface below ground level. Where this depth is less than about 6 m, the cylinder can be in the pump stand, connected to a rising pipe and foot valve in the water. Where the depth to the water surface is greater than 6 m, the cylinder must be placed below the pump stand, either in the water or not more than 6 m above it, and connected to the pump stand by a drop pipe.

If it is required to raise water to a point above the pump stand, a version of this pump known as the lift and force pump is used, in which the spout is replaced by a delivery pipe. For this version a water seal is needed at the top of the pump stand, and a linkage arrangement for the handle which keeps the pump rod moving vertically without lateral movement.

The output of a hand pump is directly related to the energy capacity of its operator. While a human being can generate quite considerable energy in short bursts, the average output for prolonged work is 0.1 to 0.08 horsepower, and 0.08 horsepower is usually taken as the operator input for a hand pump. Energy is lost in working against friction in the pump and the ratio of available power to input power is known as the efficiency of the pump, often expressed as a percentage. A usual efficiency for handpumps is 60%, so that the available power is about 0.05 horsepower.

The power used in lifting water is given by the equation:-

$$\text{Horsepower} = \frac{(\text{Flow in l/s}) \times (\text{Lift in m})}{76.1}$$

Thus for a hand pump with 0.05 available horse power, Flow x Lift = 3.8, approximately. For a lift of 1 m, delivery would be 3.8 l/s, for a lift of 20 m, delivery would be 0.2 l/s.

Despite its relatively simple mechanism, the hand-operated reciprocating pump has had a poor record of performance in a number of developing countries. Bangladesh is one country which has successfully adopted the reciprocating hand pump for small-scale irrigation. With assistance from UNICEF, a hand pump programme for shallow groundwater, known as MOSTI (Manually Operated Shallow Tubewell for Irrigation) was evolved, which included a simple borehole which could be driven by manual labour and a hand pump for irrigating an average of 0.2 ha of rice or 0.25 ha of dryland crops. The MOSTI system was introduced in the late 1950s and by 1976 there were 60,000 units in use. The cost of the installation in 1976 was US$70. The pump finally adopted for this programme, known as the 'New No.6' (Figure 48) is a cross between the USAID 'Batelle' pump and an earlier locally manufactured pump.

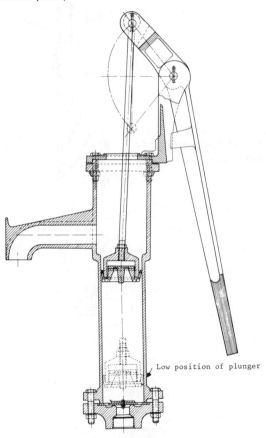

Low position of plunger

Fig.48 New No.6 hand pump (Bangladesh)

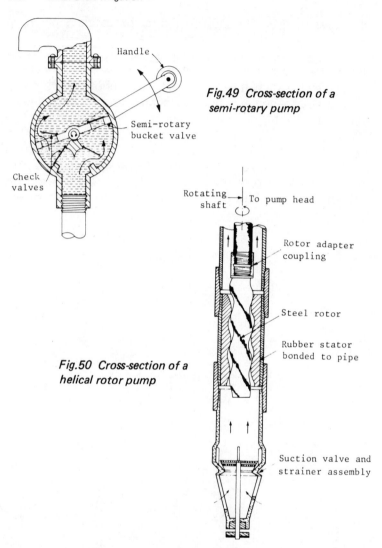

Handle

Fig.49 Cross-section of a semi-rotary pump

Semi-rotary bucket valve

Check valves

Rotating shaft — To pump head

Rotor adapter coupling

Steel rotor

Rubber stator bonded to pipe

Fig.50 Cross-section of a helical rotor pump

Suction valve and strainer assembly

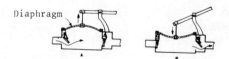

Diaphragm

A   B

Fig.51 Cross-section of a diaphragm pump

Other types of hand pump which are available include the semi-rotary and helical rotor pumps (Figures 49, 50) and the diaphragm pump (Figure 51).

Animal-powered Systems

Animal power has been used for water lifting in parts of the world for many centuries. One of the most common methods is the Persian Wheel or Saqia, which takes different forms, but they all comprise a water wheel or a chain of buckets, operated by an animal harnessed to a beam which rotates in a horizontal circle to provide the motive power (Figures 52, 53). Another use of animal power which originated in India (sometimes called the Mot) is illustrated in Figures 54 and 55. It is usually assumed that an animal working on a circular track can exert a force of one tenth of its weight at a speed of 0.7 metres per second. For an ox weighing 400 kg this is equivalent to an output of 0.4 horse-power.

Fig.52 Persian wheel ('saqia') at Dendera, Egypt (Photo: Douglas Dickins)

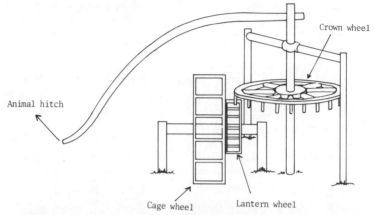

Crown wheel

Animal hitch

Cage wheel   Lantern wheel

Fig.53 Details of Persian wheel (Illustration: James Goodman)

Fig.54 Indian 'mot' at Isle of Djerba, Tunisia (Photo: Douglas Dickins)

Water Power

The energy of flowing water is used for raising water, as in the water wheel (Figure 56) and the hydraulic ram or hydram (Figures 57, 58). Water wheels are common in countries in the Far East, and can be used where there is a fairly constant flow in a river or large canal. The hydraulic ram is a self-acting pump in which a stream of water falling through a small height

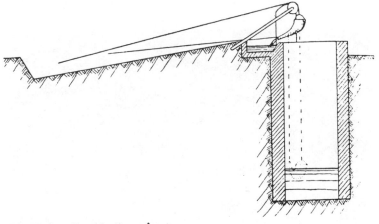

Fig.55 Details of Indian môt

raises a portion of the water to a greater height. The rate of delivery will depend upon the supply available, the working head and the height to be lifted. If a supply of 20 l/s were used with a fall of 5 metres, a delivery of 1 l/s could be raised to a height of 60 metres.

Fig.56 Water wheel on the Nile near Juba, Sudan

Fig.57   ITDG low-cost Hydraulic Ram

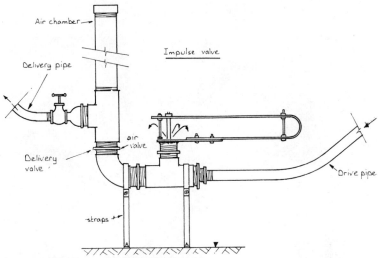

Fig.58 Details of ITDG hydraulic ram

Wind Power

The use of wind power for irrigation is practised in many countries. Commercial wind-pumps as developed in Europe, the United States and Australia, have a reputation for long service and reliable performance when adequately maintained. They are, however, expensive for the small-scale farmer, and tend to suffer from the usual problems of mechanical equipment which is dependent upon imported materials and components. Research is now being undertaken for the production of a low cost windmill, more suited to the developing country situation (Figure 59).

Mechanical Pumps

A very wide range of mechanical pumps is available to the irrigation farmer, and there is no doubt that under many conditions a mechanically-powered pump is the answer to the problem of lifting water. To describe these is beyond the scope of this book, and the reader should consult the appropriate technical works on this subject.

Further Reading

Volunteers in Technical Assistance, 'Water Lifting and Transport', *Using Water Resources,* VITA, 3706 Rhode Island Avenue, Mt. Rainer, Maryland, 20822 USA, 1977.

Fig.59 Low-cost windmill

F. Eugene McJunkin, *Hand Pumps,* Technical Paper No.10, International Reference Centre for Community Water Supply, P.O. Box 140, 2260 AC Leidschendam, The Netherlands, 1977.

S.B. Watt, *A Manual on the Hydraulic Ram for Pumping Water,* Intermediate Technology Publications Ltd, 9 King Street, London WC2E 8HN, U.K., 1977.

John Boyd, *Tools for Agriculture,* Intermediate Technology Publications Ltd, 9 King Street, London WC2E 8HN, 1976, pp.93-101.

Orson W. Israelsen, *Irrigation Principles and Practices,* John Wiley and Sons, New York, USA, 1958, Ch.5.

N.B. Webber, *Fluid Mechanics for Engineers,* Chapman and Hall Ltd, 11 New Fetter Lane, London EC4P 4EE, England, Ch.10, pp.252-263.

P.L. Fraenkel, *The Power Guide: A Catalogue of Small Scale Power Equipment,* Intermediate Technology Publications Ltd, 9 King Street, London WC2E 8HN, U.K., 1979.

Appendix A Units, Abbreviations and Conversion Factors

To convert *from* the unit column multiply *by* the appropriate conversion factor.

METRIC Unit	Abbr.	Conversion Factor	ENGLISH Unit	Abbr.	Conversion Factor
Length					
millimetre	mm	0.0394 in	inch	in	25.4 mm
centimetre	cm	0.394 in		in	2.54 cm
metre (= 1,000 mm)	m	3.281 ft	foot (= 12 in)	ft	0.3048 m
	m	1.094 yd	yard (= 3 ft)	yd	0.914 m
kilometre (= 1,000 m)	km	0.621 mile	mile (= 5,280 ft) (= 1,760 yd)	—	1.609 km
Area					
square centimetre	cm^2	0.155 in^2	square inch	in^2	6.45 cm^2
square metre	m^2	10.76 ft^2	square foot	ft^2	0.0929 m^2
	m^2	1.196 yd^2	square yard	yd^2	0.836 m^2
hectare (= 10,000 m^2)	ha	2.47 ac	acre (= 43,560 ft^2)	ac	0.405 ha
square kilometre (= 100 ha)	km^2	0.386 square mile	square mile (= 640 ac)	—	2.59 km^2
Volume					
cubic centimetre	cm^3	0.061 in^3	cubic inch	in^3	16.4 cm^3
litre (= 1,000 cm^3)	l	0.220 imperial gallon	imperial gallon (= 1.20 US gallon)	—	4.55 l
	l	0.264 US gallon	US gallon (= 0.833 imperial gallon)	—	3.79 l
	l	0.0353 ft^3	cubic foot	ft^3	28.32 l
				ft^3	6.23 imperial gallon
				ft^3	7.48 US gallon
cubic metre (= 1,000 l)	m^3	35.31 ft^3		ft^3	0.0283 m^3
	m^3	1.308 yd^3	cubic yard	yd^3	0.765 m^3
			acre-foot (= 43,560 ft^3)	—	1,233.5 m^3
Weight					
gramme	g	0.0353 oz	ounce	oz	28.35 g
kilogramme (= 1,000 g)	kg	2.205 lb	pound (= 16 oz)	lb	0.454 kg
tonne (= 1,000 kg)	t	0.984 ton	ton (= 2,240 lb)	—	1.016 tonne
Velocity					
metre per second	m/s	3.281 ft/s	foot per second	ft/s	0.3048 m/s
Rate of flow					
litre per second	l/s	0.0353 ft^3/s	cubic foot per second (= 2 acre-feet per day approx.)	ft^3/s	28.32 l/s
	l/s	13.21 imperial gallon per minute			
	l/s	15.85 US gallon per minute			
cubic metre per second (= 1,000 l/s)	m^3/s	35.31 ft^3/s		ft^3/s	0.0283 m^3/s
Density					
gramme per cubic centimetre	g/cm^3	0.0361 lb/in^3	pound per cubic inch	lb/in^3	27.68 g/cm^3
kilogramme per cubic metre	kg/m^3	0.0624 lb/ft^3	pound per cubic foot	lb/ft^3	16.02 kg/m^3
Pressure					
kilogramme per square centimetre	kg/cm^2	14.22 lb/in^2	pound per square inch (psi) (= 2.31 ft water)	lb/in^2	0.0703 kg/cm^2
	kg/cm^2	0.968 atm		lb/in^2	0.068 atm
	kg/cm^2	10 m water			
atmosphere (= 1.033 kg/cm^2)	atm	14.7 lb/in^2			
Power					
kilowatt	kW	1.341 hp	horse-power (= 550 ft lb/sec)	hp	0.746kW
metric horsepower	—	0.986 hp		hp	1.014 metric horsepower

Appendix B The Measurement of Climatic Information

I. RAINFALL

Precipitation and the Hydrological Cycle

Water falls on the earth's surface in the form of snow, hail, rain, or drizzle and condenses upon it as dew. This water, known as precipitation, originates from water vapour in the atmosphere. Much of the precipitation on land areas moves over the land surface as *run-off*, collecting in streams and rivers which flow into the oceans or other water masses such as lakes and inland seas. All these water masses are continually giving up water to the atmosphere by *evaporation.* Water also evaporates from wet land surfaces, and enters the atmosphere through the *evapotranspiration* of vegetation. This movement of water from the atmosphere to the earth's surface and back to the atmosphere is known as the *hydrological cycle,* which is illustrated in Figure B1, and it is this cycle which enables life as we know it to exist.

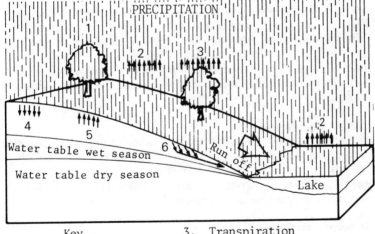

Key		3.	Transpiration
		4.	Percolation
1.	Interception	5.	Capillarity
2.	Evaporation	6.	Lateral movement

Fig.B1 Hydrological cycle under humid conditions

The amounts of precipitation which fall in the course of a year vary extensively from one place to another. Some places (deserts) have very little precipitation or none at all. Others, notably in the tropics, have a great deal. Because of these variations, and the effects which they have on agricultural practices and crop production, information about precipitation can be very useful to the farmer and cultivator.

Rainfall Records

Most inhabited areas of the world have tried to build up systematic records of rainfall, although the extent of cover, the duration of the records and the expertise available for collecting and analysing these records, vary considerably. It is unusual to find that a proposed irrigation area has been adequately surveyed and covered by systematic rain gauge records for a period long enough to assess reliable minimum, maximum and mean precipitation. This applies particularly to tropical and semi-arid areas, where variations from year to year can be very great.

Therefore as long a period as possible should be given to the investigation of a project before the design stage is reached. Frequently in practice the time factor is too short, due to the urgency of a project for which funds have been allocated. The question is, how many years' records are needed for planning irrigation? The answer depends on several factors: the urgency of the project, its size, the number of people and the investment cost likely to be involved if it fails, and the extent to which information and experience from a nearby similar development can be applied to the project. Records for 20 years are desirable, 5 years will give some idea of the rainfall characteristics of an area, and one complete year is very much better than nothing at all. Data are required on the nature and, more particularly on the amounts and timing of the precipitation and on variations in these values over the study area in which the topography may vary considerably. Rainfall is usually the most significant form of precipitation relating to irrigation projects.

Rainfall Measurement

Rainfall is measured as the depth of water falling on a horizontal surface over a period of time, which may be a day, week, month or year. It is normally measured in millimetres (one inch = 25.4 mm). Rainfall intensity is the rate at which rain falls and is expressed in units of depth (mm) per hour or per minute.

Standard Rain Gauges

The normal method of rainfall measurement in many countries is by a standard rain gauge, made of brass, copper, galvanized iron, glass fibre or plastic. It consists of a funnel which conducts the rain water to a container of 100 mm (4 inches) capacity housed in an overflow can that accommodates an additional 75 mm (3 inches) of rain. Measurements of the collected rain are made daily with a glass measuring cylinder and recorded. It is therefore necessary to employ a gauge reader who is able to record readings every 24 hours.

Less frequent measurements can be made at isolated sites where larger storage gauges are used, some with an aperture of 203 mm (8 inches) diameter, and other types even larger. One type, the 'Octapent' rain gauge, used in Britain, provides sufficient capacity for periods up to a month between observations. Figure B2 shows a British standard and an Octapent rain gauge.

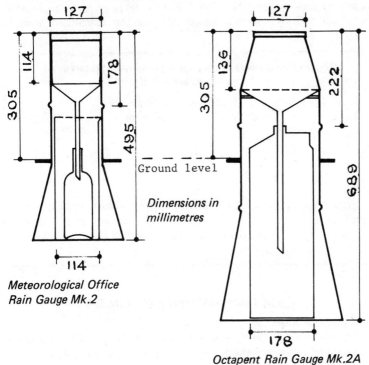

Meteorological Office
Rain Gauge Mk.2

Ground level

Dimensions in millimetres

Octapent Rain Gauge Mk.2A

Fig.B2 Two types of British rain gauges

Rainfall Recorders and Automatic Rain Gauges

Rain recorders are in use where these can be justified on scientific grounds or where daily observations are not possible. Some of these instruments record rainfall autographically on a weekly or daily chart fitted to a cylindrical drum which rotates by clockwork. The primary function of the recording gauge is to provide information about the duration and intensity of rainfall. There are many patterns of recording gauges in use in different parts of the world.

Network Design of Rain Gauge Sites

The siting network of rain gauges is important, but frequently the network is found to be quite haphazard. Probably the best way of developing the system of rain gauges is to sub-divide the area into a series of segments of uniform physiographic characteristics, and then site the gauges at points representative of these segments. A question which frequently arises concerns the number and type of rain gauges which are necessary to ensure that an accurate assessment of a catchment's rainfall is obtained. The following table gives recommended minimum densities of rain gauges for reservoir catchment areas in the UK.

Minimum numbers of rain gauges required in reservoired moorland areas (UK)

| | | Rain gauges | |
sq.km.	Daily	Monthly	Total
2	1	2	3
4	2	4	6
20	3	7	10
41	4	11	15

From 'Raingauge networks development and design with special reference to the UK', Bleasdale, World Meteorological Organisation/International Association for Scientific Hydrology Symposium, Quebec, 1965.

II. AIR TEMPERATURE AND HUMIDITY

Thermometer Readings

The Celsius (or Centigrade) scale has been adopted by the World Meteorological Organisation (WMO) and is in general use in Europe and many other parts of the world. Fahrenheit thermometers are also still used by some voluntary observers.

On the Celsius scale ($^\circ$C), the freezing point of water is zero degrees and the boiling point is 100 degrees, at standard pressure of 1013.25 millibars (mb). On the Fahrenheit scale ($^\circ$F), the freezing point of water is 32 degrees and the boiling point is 212 degrees at standard pressure. The conversion formula from Fahrenheit to Celsius scale is:

$$t\,^\circ C = \frac{5}{9} \, (t\,^\circ F - 32)$$

Air Temperature

Air temperature in the shade is recorded by thermometers housed in screens (open louvred boxes) about 1¼ metres above the ground. The screens provide protection from precipitation and the direct rays of the sun, while allowing the free passage of air. A typical screen is shown in Figure B3. Maximum and minimum thermometers record, by indices, the maximum and minimum temperatures experienced since the instruments were last set. Air temperature varies over a 24-hour day

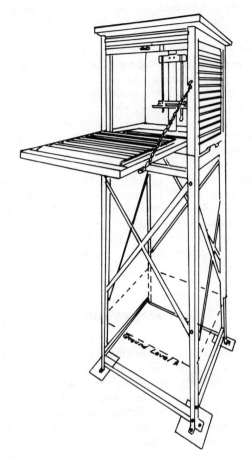

Fig.B3 Ordinary thermometer screen on steel stand

from a minimum around sunrise to a maximum from ½ to 3 hours after the sun has reached its zenith, after which there is a steady fall continuing through the night to sunrise again. Accordingly maximum and minimum observations are best made between 8 and 9 a.m.

Humidity

Absolute humidity is the quantity of water vapour in the air expressed as mass per unit volume. This quantity varies from near zero when air is very dry to a maximum, known as *saturation*, when, at a particular temperature and pressure, the air can hold no more water vapour. If saturated air is cooled, precipitation occurs: if it is warmed it starts to become unsaturated and its capacity for absorbing water vapour increases.

Relative humidity is the ratio between the actual amount of water vapour present in a volume of air to the amount which the same volume of air, at the same temperature, would hold if it were saturated. Relative humidity is usually expressed as a percentage, so that 100% refers to air which is fully saturated (at the **dew point**).

Relative humidity is measured with two thermometers, known as **wet** and **dry** bulb thermometers, placed in the screen (Figure B3). The dry bulb measures the actual air temperature. The wet bulb thermometer is identical with the dry bulb except that its bulb is covered by a piece of cloth (muslin) kept continuously wet by means of conducting threads which dip into a small container of water. The wet bulb records a lower temperature than the dry bulb owing to evaporative cooling, at all times except when the air is saturated and there is no evaporation. Then both readings will be the same. The relative humidity is obtained from the difference between the two temperatures, using specially prepared calculation tables.

III. EVAPORATION

Forms of Evaporation

Evaporation, transpiration and evapotranspiration have been defined and discussed in Chapter 9. The most common method of measuring evaporation is by means of an **evaporation pan,** which is simply a container with open top and vertical sides, with a means of measuring the water lost daily by evaporation. Many different shapes and sizes of pans are in use; some are raised above ground level, some are sunk in the ground. The most commonly used pan is the American Class A pan, made from galvanized iron, which is circular, 1.21 m diameter, 25 cm deep. The pan is mounted on a wooden open-frame platform 15 cm above ground level, and it is important that it should be accurately horizontal.

The pan is filled to a depth of 20 cm, water-level being measured by a point or hook gauge. Each day at the same time water is added to the pan (or extracted after heavy rainfall) to bring the water back to its correct depth of 20 cm. The pan observations are made in conjunction with rainfall records. If rain has fallen then allowance for this must be made in calculating the evaporation from rainfall and the amount of water added or extracted. Evaporation is recorded in millimetres of depth in a given time. The readings from a pan are known as **pan evaporation** and because the water in a pan tends to be warmer than open water in a lake, the pan evaporation has to be reduced by a **pan factor** to convert it to open water evaporation. This factor, for the

Class A pan may vary between 0.4 and 0.85 depending upon climatic conditions and geographical location. A figure often used is 0.7.

IV. SUNSHINE

Recording
The purpose of sunshine recorders is to enable the hourly or daily totals of the duration of bright sunshine to be measured accurately. The standard British instrument consists of a portion of a spherical bowl, having a glass sphere placed concentrically within it. The diameter of the bowl is such that the sun's rays are focused as sharply as possible on a card of sensitised material held inside it. The radiant heat of the sun, concentrated by the spherical lens, burns a narrow track in the specially prepared card, which is printed with blue ink, white lines and figures being left to mark the hours. Naturally the width and depth of the burn depend on how brightly the sun is shining. With a clear blue sky the card will be burned clean through; but towards sunset or just after sunrise only a faint burn will be seen under the same conditions.

Appendix C Mapping and Surveys for Irrigation

Maps are plans of the land drawn to scale showing physical features such as rivers, streams, lakes, towns, villages, roads, railways and similar information. Most maps also include information about the heights (or elevations) of some places, and many show *contour lines* (see below). Special maps are made to show special information such as vegetation, geological formations, soil types, land use and so on.

Map Scales
The scale of a map is the ratio between distances on the map and actual distances on the ground. A map sacle of 1 in 50,000 therefore means that 1 cm on the map represents 50,000 cm or 500 m on the ground. Scales of 1 in several million are used for maps of continental areas and whole countries. When larger scales are used it is convenient to print a map of a country or district in separate sheets, and a set of maps to a particular scale is known as a scale series. Thus many countries have topographical maps to the 1/250,000 series, 1/100,000 series, 1/50,000 series. For initial planning of irrigation the 1/50,000 series is useful, but for any detailed planning maps to a larger scale will be needed.

Heights on Maps
Heights on maps are referred to a *datum* or fixed base height which in most cases is *mean sea level.* By taking mean sea level as zero height,

all other heights are shown as positive when above sea level and negative when below sea level.

Contour lines are lines joining points of equal height. Contour lines are usually drawn at equal vertical intervals which may be any value from 0.25 m to 50 m, depending upon the nature of the topography and the scale of the map. When contour lines are close together, the land surface is relatively steep; when they are wide apart it is relatively flat. The slope of the land can be calculated from the spacing of contour lines. For example, if, on a 1/50,000 scale map, the distance between the contour lines representing 240 m and 245 m is 1.6 cm measured on the map, the actual distance on the ground between these lines is:

$\dfrac{1.6}{100}$ x 50,000 = 800 m. The land slope is therefore 5 m in 800 m or 1 in 40, which is a 100/40 = 2½% slope.

Contours on maps are very useful in describing the topography. Because the earth is a continuous surface, all contours must close on themselves, though not necessarily on one map sheet. Concentric contours increasing in elevation towards the centre indicate hills. Valleys normally show V- or U- shaped contours. A contour can never branch into two contours or cross another contour, and a contour line is always at right angles to the direction of maximum land slope.

Aerial Photographs

Aerial photographs are photographs of the land surface taken vertically downwards from an aeroplane flying at a constant height. They are therefore photographic maps to a scale which can be calculated from the height of the aeroplane and the optical dimensions of the camera.

Aerial photographs can be very useful for initial field planning because of their clarity and detail and because they can be used in areas previously unmapped, or mapped with insufficient detail. They are also used extensively for the preparation of topographical maps, by means of *photogrammetry,* which is the science of mapping from aerial photographs. It depends on accurate *ground control,* which means the accurate identification of points on the ground whose heights are known or can be measured, and on the skillful use of special plotting equipment.

Surveying

While existing maps may provide much useful information, it is unlikely that maps to a larger scale than 1/25,000 will normally be available, and in many countries the largest available scale is 1/50,000. A 2 hectare farm, say 200 m by 100 m would be 4 mm by 2 mm on a 1/50,000 map or 8 mm by 4 mm on a 1/25,000 map. At these scales it is unlikely that, if contours are plotted, they will be closer than at 20 or

10 metre intervals. The fall from one end of a furrow 200 m long at a 1% slope is 2 m. It will be clear therefore that these scales are not large enough for farm irrigation planning, and it will be necessary to carry out some field survey.

Field topographical survey involves making a plan of the area to be mapped, and measuring heights so that high and low points and land slopes can be identified. Heights and distance will also be required along any possible alignments from a source of water to the farm area. A suitable scale for the topographical plan may be 1/2,000, 1/1,000 or 1/500 depending on the size of the area and amount of detail required. Height measurements should be in sufficient detail to identify changes in height of not more than 0.25 m where surface irrigation is planned. For overhead irrigation, height differences of 1 m should be sufficient. The topographical survey can be made either by a *grid survey,* or by *tacheometry.* Methods of surveying will be mentioned only briefly here, and further information if needed should be sought from textbooks on survey (some references are given at the end of this Appendix).

Grid Survey

A base line is set out on the ground, usually just outside one boundary of the area to be surveyed, and a series of parallel lines (traverses) at 25 m intervals are set at right angles to the base line by compass or any other angle measuring device. The ends of the traverses and points at 25 m intervals along the traverses are fixed on the ground with wooded pegs. Distances are measured by tape or surveyor's chain.

A surveyor using a survey level with a staff and staff man, then levels along the traverses, measuring the ground level at each peg, and locating in terms of distances along each traverse, the positions of all features such as a stream, road or path, gulley, or boundary. Any important features on the ground which are not included on a traverse can be located and levelled by a measured "offset" (at a right angle) from the traverse. Wherever possible the compass bearing of the base line is noted so that the plan can be given a north point.

The result of this survey work is then plotted and the picture of the area begins to take shape. Any specific detailed survey required, such as the site of a stream diversion, the alignment of the supply channel and sites for any other structures which may be needed, will also be carried out. The channel alignment is plotted as a *longitudinal profile* showing the rise and fall of the ground surface along the alignment and the position of any significant features.

Tacheometry

A tacheometer is a theodolite equipped with means for measuring heights and distances optically by sighting and reading a staff. It is much quicker than grid surveying by direct measurement and levelling, and with care and skill can be as accurate.

Simple Survey Equipment

While surveying with the use of instruments such as surveyor's levels and theodolites is desirable because of speed and accuracy, it may not always be feasible to use them, or necessary to survey with so much detail or accuracy. Various simple devices can be made using either a suspended weight, a spirit level or two connected columns of water to establish a horizontal line. The horizontal line can be set out on the ground by sighting along pegs or vertical rods, and ground heights can be measured with reference to this horizontal datum. An irrigation supply channel planned to follow a contour line can be set out in this way. (For further information on these techniques see Ref.2)

Bench Marks

Bench marks are points of known elevation established as reference points for surveys. Permanent bench marks are established by a country's Survey Department and their locations and heights are usually marked on survey maps. A temporary bench mark is established as a local reference point for a particular survey. It may be related by levelling to a permanent bench mark, or if there is no permanent bench mark in the vicinity, it may be given an arbitrary value (such as 100.00 m).

References

1. A. Bannister and S. Raymond, *Surveying*, Pitman Publishing, Bath UK 1972.
2. John Collett and John Boyd, *Eight Simple Surveying Levels,* Intermediate Technology Publications Ltd., 9 King Street, London WC2E 8HN, UK, 1977.

Appendix D The Measurement of a Water Source

Units of Measurement

Water is measured in two ways, by *volume* and by *discharge* (or rate of flow). The international units of measurement follow the metric system (based on the centimetre, gramme, second) but American and British systems (based on the foot, pound, second) are used in many places. Units and conversion factors are given in Appendix A.

The units of volume commonly used in irrigation are the *cubic metre (m³)* and the *acre-foot,* which is the quantity of water required to cover one acre of land to a depth of one foot. One acre-foot = 1233.47 m³.

The units of discharge are the *cubic metre per second (m³/s or cumec),* the *litre per second (l/s)* and the *cubic foot per second (ft³/s or cusec).* One cusec flowing for 24 hours is approximately 2 acre-feet.

The relationship between volume and discharge in a channel or pipe is expressed by the formula $Q = AV$ where:-

Q = the discharge in m^3/s (or ft^3/s)
A = the cross-sectional area of flow in m^2 (or ft^2)
V = the mean velocity of flow in m/s (or ft/s)

Stream-flow Measurement

The principal methods of measuring stream-flow are by floats, current meters, weirs and Parshall flumes. The float method is the simplest and easiest to use, and is suitable where great accuracy is not required. Current meters are expensive instruments not likely to be available outside scientific departments or organisations, and their use will not be described here. Both weirs and flumes require more skill in their construction, but once installed they are not difficult to use by anyone familiar with the use of calibration tables or charts.

Floats

To use floats a relatively straight reach of a channel 20 to 30 m long with a fairly uniform cross section along its length is selected. Several measurements of width and depth are taken in the reach to arrive at an average cross-section area. A string or tape is stretched at right angles across the stream at each end of the reach and the distance between the strings is measured. A small float, which may be a cork, a rubber ball, or a piece of wood, is placed in the centre of the channel 1 or 2 m upstream of the start of the measured length, and the time taken to cover the measured distance is noted. This should be done three or four times to obtain an average reading. The distance divided by the time gives the velocity of the float, which corresponds to the velocity of the water at its surface. The surface velocity is multiplied by a coefficient to give the average velocity over the cross-section. This coefficient varies from 0.66 for water depths less than 30 cms to 0.80 for depths of 6 m and over. A figure of 0.7 is often used for small streams.

Thus, if the measured length is 24 m and the average time to cover this is 20 seconds the average velocity will be 0.7 x 24/20 = 0.84 m/s. If the average cross-section is 0.2 m^2, the flow (Q = AV) will be 0.2 x 0.84 = 0.168 m^3/s or 168 l/s.

To reduce the effects of wind on the floats, a method practised in India and Malaysia uses a wooden rod or tube 25 to 50 mm in diameter as a float. The rod or tube is weighted at one end and so floats vertically with a minimum surface to be affected by the wind. Alternatively a bottle, half filled with water, will serve the same purpose.

Weirs

Weirs, among the oldest and most reliable structures for measuring the flow of water in canals, ditches and streams, are overflow structures built across open channels. The discharge of the channel concerned can be determined in relation to the depth of water flowing over the weir crest. Weirs are mainly of use in measuring comparatively low discharges to obtain data, for example, for a proposed irrigation scheme, where information is required of minimum or dry weather flow. Such information will assist in deciding if the direct flow will be adequate for irrigation or if it will be necessary to dam the stream to provide storage. A weir may also be installed on an irrigation supply canal to check the actual supply discharge.

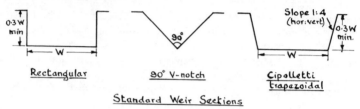

Standard Weir Sections

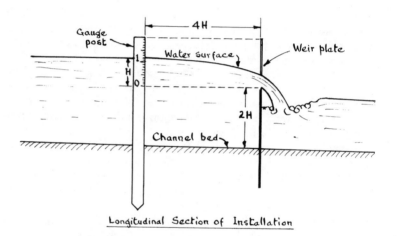

Longitudinal Section of Installation

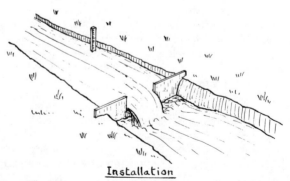

Installation

Fig.D1 Measuring weirs

Weirs usually used for flow measurement and described here are *sharp-crested, fully-contracted* and *free-flowing.* A sharp crest comprises a thin plate tapered to an edge not more than 2 mm wide. Fully contracted means that the weir has an approach channel whose bed and sides are sufficiently far from the weir crest to have no significant influence on the flow. A free-flowing weir is one where the downstream water level is below the crest. Three common types of weir are the rectangular, the 90° V-notch and the Cipolletti trapezoidal, and these weirs are illustrated in Figure D1.

Because of the effect of 'draw-down' at the crest, the water depth (H) above the crest is measured upstream of the weir, at a distance equal to 4H. This water depth is usually recorded once or twice a day, and more frequently during flood peaks, and the discharge is calculated from a formula, or read from a calibration table or chart.

Rectangular Weir

The rectangular weir consists of a horizontal crest with vertical sides. The width to height ratio of the opening should be at least 3:1. For fully-contracted conditions the difference between the width of the approach channel and the width of the weir should be at least four times the head on the crest, and the depth from the crest to the bed of the approach channel should be at least twice the head on the crest. Under these conditions the flow is given by the formula:-

$$Q = 1.84 (L - 0.2H) H^{1.5}$$

where

Q = flow in m^3/s

L = length of crest in m

H = head on crest in m

Table D1 gives flows in l/s for a standard contracted rectangular weir. The equivalent discharge formula in English units is $Q = 3.33 (L - 0.2H) H^{1.5}$ where Q is in ft^3/s, L in ft and H in ft.

90° V-notch Weir

This is an accurate flow measuring device suited for small flows. The crest of the weir consists of a V-notch, each side being inclined at 45° from the vertical. For fully contracted conditions the minimum distances of the sides of the weir from the channel banks at maximum water level should be at least twice the vertical head on the weir, and the minimum height from the bed of the pool to the point of the V should be at least twice the head on the weir.

The flow over the weir is calculated from the formula $Q = 1.368 H^{2.5}$, where H is the depth of water above the apex of the triangular V, in metres, and Q is in m^3/s. Table D2 gives flows in l/s for a small 90° V-notch weir. The equivalent discharge formula in English units is $Q = 2.49 H^{2.5}$, where Q is in ft^3/s and H is in ft.

Table D1 — Flows for standard rectangular weirs (l/s)

Head (H) cm.	Length of crest (L) cm.							
	25	50	75	100	125	150	175	200
1	0.5	0.9	1.4	1.8	2.2	2.7	3.2	3.6
1.5	0.8	1.7	2.5	3.3	4.2	5.0	5.9	6.7
2	1.3	2.6	3.9	5.1	6.4	7.7	9.0	10
3	2.3	4.7	7.1	9.5	12	14	17	19
4	3.6	7.2	11	14.5	18	22	26	29
5	4.9	10	15	20	25	31	36	41
6	6.4	13	20	27	33	40	47	54
8	9.7	20	30.5	41	51	62	72	83
10	13	28	42 .	57	72	86	100	115
12	17	36	56	75	94	113	132	151
14	21	46	70	94	118	142	166	190
16		55	85	114	143	173	202	232
18		65	100	135	170	206	241	276
20		76	117	158	199	240	281	322
25			161	218	276	333	391	448
30			208	284	359	435	511	586
35				354	449	544	640	735
40				428	544	660	777	893
45				505	644	783	921	1,060
50				585	747	910	1,072	1,235

Table D2 — Flows for a Small 90° V-notch weir (l/s)

Head cm	Flow l/s
5	0.8
6	1.1
7	1.7
8	2.5
9	3.3
10	4.3
11	5.5
12	6.8
13	8.3
14	10.0
15	11.9
16	14.0

Cipolletti Trapezoidal Weir

As its name implies, the sides of this weir are inclined instead of being vertical as in the rectangular weir. The standard side slope is 1 (horizontal) to 4 (vertical). The conditions for full contraction mentioned under the rectangular weir apply also to the trapezoidal weir. The flow of the standard Cipolletti weir is calculated from the formula:

$$Q = 1.86LH^{1.5}$$

where

Q = flow in m³/s
L = length of crest in m
H = head on crest in m.

Table D3 gives flows in l/s for a standard contracted Cipolletti trapezoidal weir. The equivalent discharge formula in English units is $Q = 3.75LH^{1.5}$ where Q is in ft³/s, L in ft and H in ft.

Table D3 — Flows for standard Cipolletti trapezoidal weirs (l/s)

Side slope 1 (Horizontal)/4 (vertical)

Head (H) cm.	Length of crest (L) cm							
	25	50	75	100	125	150	175	200
1	0.5	0.9	1.4	1.8	2.3	2.7	3.2	3.7
1.5	0.9	1.7	2.6	3.4	4.2	5.1	5.9	6.8
2	1.3	2.6	3.9	5.2	6.5	7.8	9.2	10.5
3	2.4	4.8	7.2	9.6	12	14	17	19
4	3.7	7.4	11	15	18.5	22	26	30
5	5.2	10	16	21	26	31	36	42
6	6.8	14	21	27	34	41	48	55
8	10.5	21	32	42	53	63	74	84
10	15	29	44	59	73	88	103	118
12	19	39	58	77	97	116	135	155
14	24	49	73	97	122	146	170	195
16		60	89	119	149	178	208	238
18		71	106	142	177	212	248	284
20		83	125	166	208	249	291	333
25			174	232	290	349	407	465
30			229	305	382	458	535	611
35				391	481	577	674	770
40				477	588	705	823	941
45				571	701	842	982	1,122
50					822	986	1,150	1,314

Compound Weir

In some natural streams the range of flow may be such that a V-notch is desirable for measuring very low flows, whilst a rectangular weir is more suitable for higher flows. A compound weir, consisting of a V-notch in the centre of a rectangular weir will meet this requirement. The rectangular weir portion may also consist of one or more sections of different widths, increasing with height. The total flow of a compound weir may be calculated approximately by treating each section independently and adding the results together.

Parshall Flumes

The Parshall flume, (Figure D2), named after the person who developed it, is a specially shaped open rectangular channel or flume comprising three principal sections: a converging section, leading to a constriction or throat and thence to a diverging section. The bed of the

converging section is horizontal, the bed of the throat slopes downwards
and the bed of the diverging section upwards. Water level gauges are
placed at prescribed positions in the converging section and near the

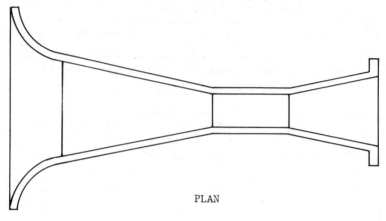

PLAN

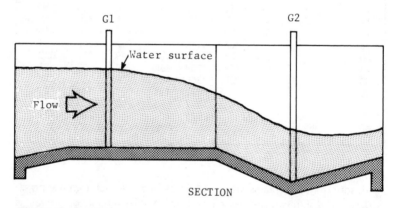

SECTION

Fig.D2 Parshall flume

downstream end of the throat. Under free flowing conditions, meaning,
in this case, when the flow through the flume is free and independent
of water level in the channel downstream of the flume, the flow is
determined from the first water level gauge (G1 in Figure D2). Under
submerged conditions, when water backs up to submerge the throat,
the second gauge (G2) is also read, and the ratio of the readings G1:G2
gives the degree of submergence. Where the submergence is greater
than 60 to 70% (depending on the size of the flume) the discharge as
calculated from G1 is corrected by a factor. At 95% submergence the
flume ceases to be effective.

The Parshall flume has a number of significant advantages. It can operate with relatively small head loss; about a quarter of the head lost with a weir. It is relatively insensitive to the velocity of approach and when properly constructed it is accurate, even when running submerged. The velocity of flow is high enough virtually to eliminate sediment deposit in the structure.

Parshall flumes have been designed in a range of standard sizes from 25 mm to 1.5 m throat widths for flows ranging from 1 l/s to over 100 m^3/s. Each flume size has a calibration table and corrections for submergence.

Springs

The yield of a spring is best measured by timing the filling of a bucket or drum of known capacity. If it takes 30 seconds to fill a 5-litre drum, then the yield is 5/30 or 1/6 l/s. Where the whole of the spring emerges at one point at which the container can be filled, measurement is easy. But often a spring seeps slowly from the ground in a number of places, and the flow needs to be concentrated to a point where it can be collected and measured.

Wells and Boreholes

The basic procedure for testing the yield from wells and boreholes is to lower the standing water level by baling or pumping, and observing the time taken for the water to recover its level. The quantity of water removed from the well by baling or pumping will be the same as the quantity required to replace it. This quantity, divided by the time of recovery will give an approximate figure for the yield, sufficiently accurate for most purposes. The yield of many wells and boreholes varies with the season of the year, and this should be taken into account.

The quantity of water extracted during the test can be measured in containers outside the well, or, in the case of a hand-dug well with a regular cross-section, by multiplying the area of the cross section by the change in water level. If, for example, the water level is lowered 2 m in a circular well 1.3 m diameter, the volume of water removed will be:-

$$\frac{\pi}{4} \times (1.3)^2 \times 2 = \frac{3.1416 \times 1.69}{2}$$

$$= 2.65 \text{ m}^3$$

If it takes 4 hours for this water level to recover, the yield of the well is:-

$$\frac{2.65}{4} = 0.663 \text{ m}^3/\text{h}$$

or

$$\frac{663}{3600} = 0.18 \text{ l/s}$$

This well would yield 0.18 l/s continuously for 24 hours a day. If it were intended to use it for irrigation, drawing water for 10 hours a day, water could be extracted at a higher rate, depending upon the storage capacity of the well. Suppose there is no water left when the level is lowered 2 m at the end of the day, and during the night the water level rises 2 m ready for watering the next morning. The total amount of water which can be extracted in 10 daytime hours will be the yield in 10 hours plus the storage volume, and this amounts to:-

$$10 \times 0.663 + 2.65 = 8.28 \text{ m}^3$$

This is equivalent to a yield of 0.828 m³/h or 0.23 l/s during this time.

The yield of a borehole can be measured in the same way by pumping to lower the level, and timing the recovery. If, as is usually the case, the standing water level is 50 m or more below ground level, it is not easy to measure this depth without special equipment. The water removed is measured as it is pumped out. With a low-yielding borehole served by a hand pump this can be done by filling containers. With higher yields and delivery by mechanical pump, the quantity extracted is best measured by a flow-meter or portable channel and weir.

References

1. Development and Resources Corporation, *Irrigation Principles and Practices,* P & T Journal No.5, United States Peace Corps. 806 Connecticut Ave., Washington, DC 20525, USA, 1969 (Reprint 1976), pp.41-50.
2. Food and Agriculture Organization of the United Nations, *Small Hydraulic Structures,* Irrigation and Drainage Paper 26/2, Land and Water Development Division, FAO, Via delle Terme di Caracalla, 00100 Rome, Italy, 1975, Section 7.

Appendix E Two Case Studies in Management

I. COMMUNAL IRRIGATION SYSTEMS IN THE PHILIPPINES

Adapted from a paper presented at the Water Management Workshop at the International Rice Research Institute, the Philippines, in December 1972 entitled "Organisation and Operation of 15 Communal Irrigation Systems in the Philippines" by P.S. Ongkingco.

About thirty per cent of the more than one million hectares of irrigation land in the Philippines is served by communal system. A communal irrigation system includes the characteristics of being small in size, usually less than 1,000 ha, basically inexpensive and projects in which farmer beneficiaries provide financial and labour inputs during the system construction. Also, the systems are operated and maintained by the farmers on a self-financing basis. Frequently some sort of farmers' association exists to administer and maintain the scheme. Maintenance costs may either be met by a system of payments, for example one sack (normally 44 kg) of rough rice per hectare per year for the water used, or the farmers may undertake the weeding and repair of the canals themselves when necessary. In some cases farmers co-operate voluntarily without a formal association.

Communal Problems

Once the communal irrigation system has been established, there are normally two main problems which affect its satisfactory operation. The one which is perhaps most likely to produce discord amongst the farmers is the problem of ensuring a fair distribution of water to all. This factor frequently results in dissatisfaction and conflict, particularly within schemes for which the water supply is inadequate to meet all the farmers' needs. The other main problem arises out of the need for adequate and prompt maintenance of the canals, which in turn can affect the first problem, the fair distribution of water.

In 1972 there were at least 16 communal systems in the province of Laguna, which lies about 70 km to the south of Manila around the southern end of lake Laguna de Bay. Most of these communal systems received some initial assistance, notably from the National Irrigation Administration (NIA) or the Presidential Assistance on Community Development (PACD), both of which are Philippine government organisations. Their sizes range from 14 to 1300 hectares, for a total of 4570 hectares through the province. The assistance given was either grants for basic materials such as cement and steel, or technical assistance for design and the supervision of construction, or both.

In many of the schemes the distribution of water and weeding and repairing of canals is made the responsibility of one person, often called a *ditch tender* or *water master*, who may be paid, for example, a certain weight of rice per year by each of the farmers served. In some cases, such as the Prinza Irrigation Dam System, Calavan, the ditch tender may not be able to do all the work alone and so may have to hire labour on his own account. At the Prinza scheme his twelve years of service as ditch tender affords him sufficient experience to be able to advise the farmers on such questions as the times to spray against pests, or apply fertilizer. The farmers whom he serves also come to him regarding their problems in water delivery and schedule and his decisions are respected because he was appointed by the mayor.

Other systems, particularly the smaller ones, have no formal farmers' organisation, or *ditch tender.* The work of cleaning and repairing irrigation canals is done by the farmers but under the direction of an official. In the case of the 60 hectare Pangil system, this official is the vice-mayor, a farmer-land-owner in the system, who also leads the campaign to kill rats which attack the rice plants.

The position of *water master* to the 40-farmer Dalitiwan system at Majayjay is unpaid and was inherited from his father and grandfather before him. Originally it was "given" to his family because they were the owners of the largest rice farm (3 hectares). When repairs or maintenance of the canals are needed, the *water master* tells the farmers where and at what time to report to do the work.

Some systems apparently have no *water master* or official permanently in charge of the distribution of water and of maintenance of the canals. When the water supply is insufficient, it is divided by the farmers amongst their farms, in some systems on a rotation basis. However, many of the farmers on such systems, for example the Cortadilla and Mayputat systems at Santa Maria, whose land is furthest away from the main canal, say that the water distribution is unfair.

Within the municipality of Magdalena there are two systems which together irrigate about 170 hectares. After one unusually dry season, the town mayor, anticipating conflict between farmers over the abstraction of water from the system, assigned a policeman to help distribute the limited supply with occasional supervision by himself. The farmers appreciated this action even when they were allocated water only 2 days a week.

Technical Problems

In order to try to ensure that farmers' rice yields are not depressed due to lack of water, it is important to make certain (if possible) that the supply to the communal irrigation system is adequate to fulfil the needs of all the farms. If this can be achieved, then the chances of conflict between members over the distribution of water will also be reduced.

If the total annual quantity of water available from the surplus is insufficient, there may be little that the farmers' association or its members may be able to do, but there are situations where action can be taken to improve the position.

The Niugan system at Cabuyao serves about 500 hectares during the rainy season, but only about 10-20 hectares during the dry season due to low water supply. Some enterprising farmers have installed tube wells to assure an adequate water supply in both seasons of the year. Some even provide water to nearby farms, for a fee.

Technical and financial assistance to the farmers' association of the Santo Angel system enabled them to construct a concrete dam to replace the earlier brushwood dam, which was unable to provide a satisfactory water supply. Now all the fields of the 120 hectare system can be well irrigated since leaks in the original dam have been eliminated, assuring the farmers of a twice-a-year harvest of 3.2 to 3.5 t/ha. In addition, the farmers are now relieved of repairing the dam every time there is a flood. However, since the completion of the new dam the farmers' association has become inactive, the members pay no fee, and there are no reserves to pay for repairs and maintenance.

Conclusions

To sum up, some of the main problems which those communal systems have met, and for which solutions are needed:

a. equitably sharing the water supply,
b. sharing the task of canal maintenance,
c. overcoming technical problems in the water supply.

Sharing water and tasks of maintenance are achieved most satisfactorily where this is under the control of a respected member of the local community, who may or may not be paid for his services. In the Philippines, a local government officer such as mayor or vice-mayor, even if he is also an irrigating farmer, carries enough weight to be acceptable as an arbitrator. This would not apply in many countries.

II. FAIR DISTRIBUTION IN BALI

Reprinted from The New Scientist 17th November 1977.

The Balinese evolved what is probably the most socially sophisticated system of village irrigation anywhere in the world. Every owner of land in a particular ecological unit — watered by the same stream or canal — belongs to a common organisation, the sebak, which maintains the system and controls water use. It meets once every Balinese month of 35 days, and has its own system of law called awigawig. Every landowner has to provide free labour one day a month for repair and maintenance — the more land he owns, the more labour he must provide or pay for.

The sebak decides democratically on planting times — simultaneous planting is preferred to keep pests and diseases down, but if water is insufficient for everyone's land to be irrigated at the same time, the sebak works out a complicated planting and cropping rota to stagger the demand for water. Though landholding is far from equal, water is distributed with scrupulous fairness. Its supply is regulated into each parcel of land by a length of coconut tree trunk spanning the inlet. For every one tenah of land (0.35 hectares) he owns, each sebak member has a right to one tektek of water. A tektek is a gap four fingers wide cut into the coconut trunk. Anyone who attempts to cheat the system, and take more water than he is entitled to, can be tried by the sebak meeting and fined heavily.

The technology of the system is as primitive as its organisation is advanced. The weirs are just piles of stones in the rivers. The coconut trunk inlet regulates only the width of water, not the height. In the heavy rains of November and December flash floods often sweep away weirs and break down the bundhs between fields. Farmers usually delay planting for as much as two months, until water supply is more even. That delay costs an extra crop of rice in most areas.

In Bali the small-scale irrigation effort has gone into upgrading the village systems — building permanent, solid weirs and primary canals and providing control gates that can regulate the supply of water. Areas that have already been upgraded have seen an increase in cropping intensity of anything up to 80 per cent.

In all the small-scale irrigation projects labour-intensive methods are used. Excavation, even of long tunnels, is by pick and shovel; waste is carried away in straw baskets on the head. Masonry is used instead of concrete; and the stones are collected and broken up on or near the site. One Balinese weir was getting the final touches when I saw it — workers were handsetting thousands of tiny pebbles into mortar to provide an attractive finish.